"Cooking with Love provides food for the Soul" ♡

THE COMPLETE

KitchenAid®
Stand Mixer
COOKBOOK

Publications
International, Ltd.

Recipe development on pages 13, 86, 92, 100 and 164 by Bianca Gatti; on pages 46 and 90 by Carissa Kinyon; on pages 18, 72, 106 and 124 by Marilyn Pocius; on pages 20, 44, 50, 62, 64, 74, 78, 88, 96, 98, 120, 142, 150, 172 and 174 by Rick Rodgers.

Photography on pages 19, 21, 42, 45, 46, 51, 63, 65, 73, 74, 79, 87, 89, 91, 93, 97, 99, 101, 105, 107, 121, 125, 143, 150, 165, 173, 174 and 179 by PIL Photo Studio, Chicago.

Photographers: Justin Paris, Annemarie Zelasko
Photographers' Assistant: Tony Favarula
Food Stylists: Mary Ann Melone, Walter Moeller, Josephine Orba
Assistant Food Stylists: Lisa Dumstorff, Elaine Funk, Bianca Gatti, Sheila Grannen, Lissa Levy, Breanna Moeller

Pictured on the front cover: French Macarons *(pages 166—170)*.

Pictured on the back cover *(top to bottom):* Exotic Veggie Chips *(page 124)*, Butternut Squash Ravioli with Sage Butter *(page 50)* and Lamb, Feta & Sun-Dried Tomato Sausages *(page 64)*.

Contributing Writer: Marilyn Pocius

ISBN-13: 978-1-4508-5840-3
ISBN-10: 1-4508-5840-6

Library of Congress Control Number: 2012938837

Manufactured in China.

8 7 6 5 4 3 2 1

contents

Getting the Most from Your KitchenAid® Stand Mixer

You count on your KitchenAid stand mixer to mix cookies, whip egg whites and knead bread dough, but there are countless other ways it can make cooking and baking easier, better and more enjoyable. Every stand mixer comes with three basic attachments: the flat beater, wire whip and dough hook. Here are some tips on making the best use of all three.

 ## Flat Beater

The flat beater is probably the attachment you use most. It's perfect for creaming butter and sugar, combining ingredients, beating cake batters and many other basic tasks. Use it for: cakes, creamed frostings, candies, cookies, pie pastry, biscuits, quick breads, meat loaf and mashed potatoes.

SPEED TO SPARE

Your KitchenAid stand mixer will mix faster and more thoroughly than most other mixers. When converting traditional recipes, bear in mind that times must be adjusted to avoid overbeating. With cakes from scratch, for example, beating time may be half as long as with other mixers. (For more on converting recipes, see your KitchenAid stand mixer instruction and recipe book.)

Cutting Butter or Shortening into Flour

Your KitchenAid stand mixer makes short work of short doughs, including biscuits, pie pastry and scones without overworking the dough. Cut chilled butter or shortening into pieces and add it to the flour in the mixer bowl. Turn the flat beater to low and mix until the mixture resembles coarse crumbs (or the texture specified for a particular recipe). You'll keep your hands clean and the butter cold, which makes for a lighter flakier result.

 ## Wire Whip

The wire whip is the attachment to reach for when air needs to be incorporated into a mixture. This includes recipes that call for beaten egg whites, like soufflés, angel food cakes, sponge cakes and French macarons. The whip is also perfect for making mayonnaise or boiled frostings and, of course, for whipping cream.

How to Whip Egg Whites

It's easiest to separate egg yolks from whites when the eggs are cold, however, room temperature whites achieve greater volume. Be careful to keep all of the yolk, or any other fat, out of the egg whites. A drop or two of yolk is enough to prevent proper whipping.

Place the room temperature whites in a clean, dry mixer bowl. (Even a tiny bit of leftover

4

grease in the bowl could prevent the whites from achieving volume.) Attach the wire whip. Whip, gradually increasing the speed to high. Beat until the egg whites reach the desired stage.

Foamy or Frothy: Large uneven air bubbles form.

Soft Peaks: Whites form a peak when lifted, but tips fall over when the whip is removed.

Stiff, Shiny Peaks: Sharp stiff peaks remain even when the whip is removed. Egg whites are glossy.

Sweetened Whipped Cream

1 1/2 **cups heavy whipping cream**
 1/4 **cup powdered sugar**
 1/2 **teaspoon vanilla**

Place mixer bowl and wire whip in the freezer for 15 minutes to chill. Attach wire whip; pour cold whipping cream into mixer bowl. To avoid splashing, begin whipping on low and gradually increase speed to high. When cream forms soft peaks, add powdered sugar and vanilla and continue beating until the desired consistency. (Do not overbeat or cream will become grainy.)

● **MAKES ABOUT 3 CUPS. MAY BE DOUBLED.**

A CRASH COURSE IN CREAM
Labels on containers of cream can be mystifying. Here are some definitions.

Light Cream (18 to 30% butterfat): Generally the same as half-and-half. Will only whip if it contains 30% butterfat.

Whipping Cream (30% butterfat): Will whip and thicken, but not as well as heavy cream.

Heavy Whipping Cream (36 to 38% butterfat): Whips up well and holds its shape. Doubles in volume when whipped.

Pasteurized vs. Ultra-Pasteurized: Ultra-pasteurized whipping cream has been heated to a higher temperature than regular pasteurized cream in order to extend its shelf life. Ultra-pasteurized cream takes longer to whip and will not retain peaks like pasteurized cream.

WHAT IS CREAM OF TARTAR ANYWAY?
Adding an acid ingredient to egg whites helps keep the foam more stable once it's whipped. Cream of tartar is usually the suggested acid, although lemon juice or even vinegar will work. And no, cream of tartar is not a milk product or what the dentist removes when he cleans your teeth. It's sediment produced on barrels during wine making. It is also the acidic ingredient in many baking powders.

Dough Hook

The dough hook is a breadmaker's best friend. Use it for mixing and kneading yeast doughs including breads, rolls, coffee cakes and buns.

What You Knead to Know
Yeast is alive. Use a kitchen thermometer to check liquids. Temperatures that are too high can kill the yeast and low temperatures will slow yeast growth and the time required for bread to rise.

Most bread recipes call for a range in the amount of flour. You'll know you've added enough when dough clings to the hook and cleans the side of the bowl. Some dough, especially when made with whole grains, may not form a ball on the hook. As long as the hook is making contact with the dough, it is being kneaded. Always keep the speed low while using the dough hook. Refer to the stand mixer instruction book for details.

Rising times vary due to any number of factors, including the temperature and humidity level in your kitchen. To judge whether dough has doubled, press into it lightly with your fingers. If the indentations remain, the dough has risen enough.

Fresh Pasta the Easy Way

Pasta Sheet Roller and Cutters

You'll find more information, suggested roller settings and basic recipes on pages 82 through 85. Even with the same recipe, pasta dough seems to change every time you make it. It can behave differently depending on the size of the eggs, brand of flour and even the temperature and humidity in the room. Preparation instructions are included with the recipes, but here are some troubleshooting tips.

Dough Gets Crumbly When Put Through the Rollers.

Don't worry if your dough shreds a bit the first time it's fed through thickness setting 1. The Pasta Sheet Roller will help smooth it out. Fold the dough in thirds and keep rolling and feeding it through the rollers at setting 1 at least three times. Continue until it becomes smooth and pliable before moving to the next setting.

There is something very satisfying about creating a delicious dinner from not much more than humble flour and eggs. Dried packaged pasta is convenient and tasty, but it just can't compare with the flavor and texture of fresh pasta you make yourself. With KitchenAid attachments, pasta making is fun and virtually foolproof. There's no laborious kneading or tricky rolling. Invite the kids or friends to help and pasta making may be as much fun as pasta eating. Once you've mastered basic egg pasta, try fettuccine made from whole wheat or use the Pasta Sheet Roller to enclose basil leaves in your dough. (See the recipe for Basil Pasta Aglio e Olio on page 92.) The pasta possibilities are endless!

> **SEMOLINA FLOUR**
>
> Semolina flour is made from durum wheat. Durum is a hard wheat (high in protein) that is used for commercial dried pasta. Adding semolina flour to your pasta dough makes a bit firmer noodle. Be careful when purchasing semolina, however, since grain labeled just "semolina" can be a coarser grind used for porridge like farina. You need finely ground semolina flour. It's available in large supermarkets, Italian markets and online.

Dough Sticks to the Rollers.

Sprinkle flour on the piece of dough before you feed it through the rollers and on the work surface as well. Don't rush through the roller settings. Remember that setting 1 is helping to knead the dough, so keep flouring and feeding it through until it is pliable, but not sticky. (Also make sure you are at setting 1 and not at a higher, thinner setting by mistake.) Clean the rollers with a brush to remove any stuck-on dough between batches.

Dough Is Sticky and Hard to Handle.

Don't forget to let the dough rest for at least 20 minutes and up to an hour at room temperature before rolling. This gives the gluten (the stretchy protein in flour) a chance to develop and gives flour time to thoroughly absorb liquid. If you can't finish making the pasta right away, store well-wrapped dough in the refrigerator for up to three days. Let it return to room temperature before rolling.

Noodles Stick Together after Being Cut.

It helps to gently separate noodles with floured fingers as they exit the cutting blades. Fan them out on a floured kitchen towel or sheet of parchment paper. Pasta should be dried for 10 minutes before cooking it. You can hang long pasta on a pasta drying rack or over a clean towel on the back of a chair or cabinet door. If you

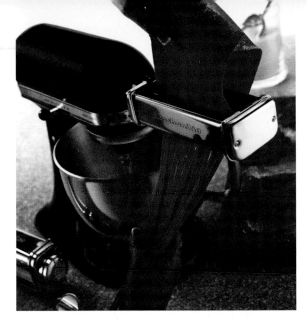

have the space, pasta can also be draped over a clean sheet spread over a counter or table. You can even improvise a pasta rack with clean coat hangers.

Pasta Breaks into Short Pieces Instead of Long Noodles.

If you are working with whole wheat or spinach pasta, it's best to choose fettuccine or another fairly wide cutter. Because of the fiber in the dough, these pastas don't cut cleanly into narrow noodles like angel hair. It's also possible that you've let the pasta sheets dry for too long and they've become brittle. Fortunately, even pasta that looks less than perfect still tastes very good!

7

STORING HOMEMADE PASTA

Once it is dry, pasta can be stored in a plastic bag or airtight container in the refrigerator where it will keep for up to three days. For longer storage, freeze pasta for up to four months. Arrange pasta on a floured piece of parchment paper on a baking sheet. To handle long pasta shapes, flour the noodles and arrange them into round nests to save space and provide convenient portions. Freeze pasta for a day until solid and then transfer it to a freezer bag or other freezer container. There's no need to defrost pasta before cooking. Just add it to boiling water and cook for a bit longer than you would for fresh.

sheets won't fill properly. Let dough sheets dry on a flat surface for 10 minutes before making ravioli.

Troubleshooting Tips

Pasta sheets need to be uniformly wide and thick to feed into the machine evenly. Trim the edges of dough if necessary beforehand and flour the sheets as needed to prevent sticking. Be careful not to add filling too quickly (usually one scoop of filling at a time with the provided spoon is enough) since it can prevent raviolis from sealing properly. Spinach or nut fillings need to be smooth purées for the same reason. Make sure all of the filling is enclosed before the end of the pasta sheet or you risk getting filling on the rollers.

Let the finished ravioli sheets dry on a lightly floured surface for 10 minutes before separating them, one by one, along the perforations. Let them dry or freeze them in a single layer to prevent sticking. Before beginning a new sheet of ravioli, brush away any dried dough from the last batch and dust the rollers with flour.

 # Ravioli Maker

Turn out dozens of picture perfect ravioli in a matter of minutes with the KitchenAid® Ravioli Maker. It fills prepared sheets of pasta and even crimps the edges. Consult the instruction book for detailed directions on using this attachment. For a ravioli dough recipe, see page 83.

Preparing the Dough Sheets.

To feed correctly through the Ravioli Maker, dough sheets should be $1/16$ of an inch thick and $5^1/_2$ inches wide. Using the Pasta Sheet Roller, this means that dough should be as wide as the rollers and rolled to thickness setting 4. Thinner dough sheets can break and leak filling. Narrower

8

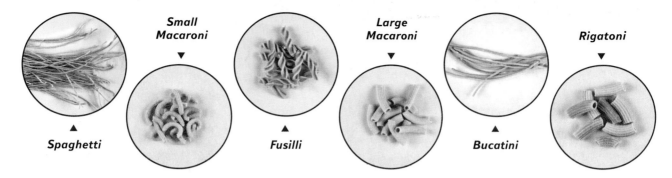

Small Macaroni ▼

▲ Spaghetti

Large Macaroni ▼

Rigatoni ▼

Fusilli

▲ Bucatini

 # Pasta Press

Now homemade rigatoni is within reach! The KitchenAid® Pasta Press attachment lets you choose from six pasta shapes. It's fast and easy. Simply attach the desired pasta plate, feed dough into the hopper and press out macaroni, fusilli, spaghetti, rigatoni and even bucatini. (Read the instruction book that comes with your Pasta Press carefully for assembly, cleaning and safety instructions.)

Because the Pasta Press extrudes dough through a die, the texture of the dough is a bit different than from dough used with the Pasta Roller and Cutter attachments. It needs to be drier and more like pie crust or biscuit dough. Recipes for Eggless Pasta Dough as well as Whole Wheat Dough for the Pasta Press are on pages 83 and 85.

Helpful Tips

The dough should be fed gradually into the hopper in walnut-sized pieces. Add additional dough after the previous pieces have disappeared into the hopper. If the first few noodles come out broken or ragged, squeeze the dough back together and return it to the hopper.

Keep the wire cutter clean of dried dough. Separate long pasta pieces gently with floured hands as they come out of the press so they don't stick together. Arrange short pasta in a single layer on a lightly floured sheet of parchment or a clean kitchen towel. Hang longer pasta from a drying rack and keep it separated. Consult the instruction book for the different extrusion speeds required for different pasta shapes.

9

COOKING PERFECT FRESH PASTA

Bringing a big pot of water to a boil to cook pasta takes time, so don't leave it to the last minute. Salting the water is not required, but can be important for flavor, especially if there is no salt in the pasta recipe itself. How much salt? There are as many answers to that question as there are Italian grandmas. For 6 quarts of water you'll need at least a few tablespoons. Add the pasta only after the water is at a full boil. Stir gently to keep the noodles from sticking together. Once the water returns to a boil, watch closely. Thin pasta can be done in one minute while thicker cuts may take five to seven minutes. The best way to know pasta is al dente and done to your liking is to remove a piece and taste it. Remember, too, that residual heat will continue cooking the pasta a bit while it drains. It's better to err on the side of slightly undercooked

Ice Cream Made Simple

 With the KitchenAid® Ice Cream Maker attachment you can create classic creamy chocolate and vanilla ice creams, custom flavors, gelatos, sorbets and more. Mix in your favorite candy, fruit or nuts. Experiment with savory flavors or exotic fruits. Try Avocado Lime Ice Cream on page 46, or Pomegranate & Orange Sherbet on page 174. There's a world of choices beyond chocolate and vanilla!

The Cold, Cold Facts

There's one important rule for making ice cream—everything must be very cold. Keep the ice cream bowl and dasher in the freezer for AT LEAST 15 hours before using it. In fact, the best way to be ready is to always store the bowl in the freezer between batches. Don't remove it until everything is set to go and your ice cream mixture is cold, too.

You can chill your ice cream mixture by refrigerating it until cold (40°F), which will take at least two hours. If you don't want to wait

---

RIPENING ICE CREAM

It's an odd word, but ripening is the term used for freezing freshly churned ice cream until firm. The consistency of just-churned ice cream is about that of soft-serve, but after an hour or two in the freezer it becomes firm enough to scoop.

(and who wants to wait for ice cream?) make an ice water bath. Nestle the prepared bowl of ice cream mixture inside a larger bowl of ice water. Let it stand for about one hour stirring occasionally, and adding ice to the bigger bowl if needed, until the mixture reaches 40°F.

Turning and Churning

It is extremely important to assemble the frozen bowl and dasher and turn your mixer on before pouring in the cold ice cream mixture. If you add it to the bowl before the dasher is turning, it can freeze immediately and cause the dasher to slip.

Always set your mixer to the lowest stir speed. Generally ice cream is ready after 20 to 25 minutes of churning, when it has reached the consistency of soft-serve ice cream. Timing does vary somewhat depending on ingredients. If the dasher begins to slip and make a clicking noise, the ice cream is done.

When mixing in solid ingredients, like candy, chocolate chips, fruit or nuts, wait until the final two minutes of the mixing process to add them.

Turn Up the Volume

Your KitchenAid® Ice Cream Maker has a larger bowl than many other machines. The yield for most recipes is 8 cups or 2 quarts. Be aware that ice cream increases in volume substantially as it churns. Never overfill the bowl or start with more than 46 ounces of liquid.

THE SCOOP ON SCOOPING

Once your ice cream is thoroughly frozen (ripened) it may be too solid to scoop right out of the freezer. Allow it to sit at room temperature for 5 to 10 minutes or help things along by microwaving it for 20 to 30 seconds on low power. Running your ice cream scoop under hot water first also helps.

Put the Rotor Slicer/Shredder to Work on Anything from Soup to Nuts

 Need to grate the Gruyère for Classic French Onion Soup (page 132)? Grind nuts for Vegetarian Nut Loaf (page 133)? Slice veggies for chips? The Rotor Slicer/Shredder attachment just may  be the most versatile tool you can use with your stand mixer. Choose the appropriate cone for the job and make quick work of what used to be tedious chores.

Always follow assembly and safety directions in the KitchenAid® Rotor Slicer/Shredder instruction book that comes with the attachment.

Which Cone for What Job?

Cones are numbered on their closed ends.

Fine Shredder (cone number 1): Use this to finely shred hard, crisp vegetables, including carrots, beets, turnips, potatoes and celery. Also good for shredding firm cold cheese, coconut and dried bread.

Coarse Shredder (cone number 2): Use this to coarsely shred carrots, celery or onions and to make coarse shredded potatoes for potato pancakes. Also shreds some fruits, nuts and chocolate.

Thick Slicer (cone number 3): Use this to thickly slice firm vegetables that are to be steamed, fried, scalloped or creamed.

Thin Slicer (cone number 4): Use this to get thin slices of vegetables for slaw, potato chips, sauerkraut, pickles and salads.

CLEAN UP TIPS

The Rotor Slicer/Shredder housing and cones are dishwasher safe. Some foods, such as carrots, may stain the housing. Remove stubborn stains by rubbing a small amount of oil over them, washing in warm sudsy water and rinsing thoroughly.

Helpful Tips

Shredding cheeses, especially soft ones like Gouda or Monterey Jack, is easier if they are very cold or even partially frozen. Place them in the freezer for 20 minutes before shredding.

Vegetables should be cut into sizes that fit in the hopper. You can use half of the hopper for narrow items like carrots by lifting the handle on just one side. If you wish to make round slices, stand the vegetable up vertically in the hopper. Remember, you can change cone sizes to handle multiple tasks without disassembling the housing.

WHY BOTHER TO SHRED CHEESE?

Packs of shredded cheese are readily available, so why take the time to shred it at home? The most obvious reason is that it's considerably more economical. Check prices on a one pound block of Cheddar versus one pound of shredded Cheddar (4 cups). Choices of packaged shredded cheese are also limited to the mainstream varieties—no Gouda or Fontina. And did you know that shredded cheese contains anticaking agents? They usually include potato starch and powdered cellulose.

11

Grind Big Jobs Down to Size with the KitchenAid® Food Grinder

No wonder the Food Grinder is one of the best selling attachments for the stand mixer: It makes quick work of burgers, falafel, sausage, pesto, salsa and much more.

Two different plates—coarse and fine—let you control the texture. The coarse plate can be used for grinding raw or cooked meats, firm vegetables, dried fruit and cheese. Use the fine plate for finer textured raw meat, cooked meat for spreads or for making bread crumbs. Food should be cut into pieces or strips that easily fit into the hopper. Always use the food pusher to feed food into the hopper.

Most salsas and relishes can be made by grinding ingredients together—no need to chop parsley or cilantro or mince garlic beforehand. Just add sprigs of herbs or peeled cloves of garlic to the hopper. The Food Grinder can handle wedges of onion or tomatillos, too. (See the recipe for Black Bean Flautas with Charred Tomatillo Salsa on page 126.) Pesto Sauce (page 76) made with the grinder has a slightly coarser texture than when it's made in a blender, more like real Italian pesto made with a mortar and pestle. See the instruction booklet for more recipe ideas as well as assembly instructions and safety precautions.

Meat Matters

With the Food Grinder, you can turn humble beef chuck into the Ultimate Grilled Burger (page 62) or make homemade breakfast sausage with your own signature spice blend. Grinding at home lets you decide on the kind, quality and cut of meat that goes into the finished product. No worries about extenders, additives or other mystery ingredients. You control the amount of fat and know exactly when it was ground. (Who knows how long supermarket ground meat has been sitting shrink-wrapped in its plastic tray.) Need more reasons? Freshly ground meat tastes better and grinding your own can save you money.

BUT WHAT'S PORK BUTT?

It's not what it sounds like! Pork butt, which is also called Boston butt, is actually pork shoulder and an excellent cut to use for sausage. It's called butt because a century or so ago, pork shoulder roasts were packed and shipped, often from Boston, in a barrel called a butt.

12

Maple Sage Breakfast Sausage

3 **pounds boneless pork shoulder (butt), cut into 2-inch strips**

1/3 **cup real maple syrup (not pancake syrup)**

1 **tablespoon kosher salt**

1 **tablespoon chopped fresh sage**

1 **teaspoon dried thyme**

1 **teaspoon red pepper flakes**

1 **teaspoon ground black pepper**

1/2 **teaspoon freshly grated nutmeg**

1 Spread pork on baking sheet. Refrigerate or freeze until slightly firm.

2 Assemble Food Grinder with coarse grinding plate. Grind pork into mixing bowl. Add remaining ingredients to mixing bowl. Replace Food Grinder with flat beater. Mix 1 minute or until well blended.

3 Shape mixture into 3-inch patties. Heat large skillet over medium heat; cook patties 3 minutes per side until browned and cooked through (160°F).

● **MAKES 8 TO 10 SERVINGS**

Tips for Smooth Grinding

Keep things cold. The easiest grinding and best texture result when meat is very cold or even partially frozen. After cutting meat into strips that will fit into the hopper of the Food Grinder, spread them in a single layer on a parchment- or foil-lined baking sheet. Refrigerate or freeze until firm. This will take 20 to 30 minutes in the refrigerator or about 15 minutes in the freezer. It's fine to use cheaper, tougher cuts of meat for sausage making. Shoulder cuts, like pork butt or beef chuck are preferred since they result in flavorful, juicy sausage. Trim any gristle or connective tissue as you cut the meat into strips.

Fat facts. Sausage needs some fat for flavor, but your homemade sausage will contain considerably less than almost any prepared product. Fresh pork fatback is usually recommended since it has a mild flavor and good texture. The term "fatback" refers to the layer of white fat that runs along a hog's back. Most butchers will be happy to sell you fatback at a reasonable price. Don't confuse fresh pork fatback with cured or smoked pork belly or salt pork, which are used for other kinds of recipes.

Be patient. Don't try to hurry the process by stuffing too much meat into the hopper or pressing down too hard on the pusher. Slow and steady keeps the meat cold and prevents the ground meat from becoming mushy or jamming the machine. Always return the seasoned ground meat to the refrigerator right after mixing it.

Links versus patties. Once ground, sausage can be formed into patties or stuffed into casings to make links. Most sausage recipes, including the ones in this book, are delicious either way. But once you experience the fun of sausage making, you'll probably want to turn it into professional looking links that are ready for the grill. With the help of the KitchenAid® Sausage Stuffer attachment for your Food Grinder, it's a lot easier than you might think.

Conquering casings. Purchasing and using sausage casings is actually fairly straightforward. Natural hog casings in a medium size are the most common since they are easy to work with and readily available. Relax! They come already cleaned and are usually packed in salt. You only have to rinse and soak the casings before use to remove the salt. Your butcher will probably sell you natural casings if you ask, or you can easily order them online. One pound of meat will use about 2 feet of casings. Unused salted casings can be refrigerated for up to a year. Vegetarian and collagen casings are also available, though a bit more difficult to work with.

Consult the Sausage Stuffer instruction book for directions on handling casings, filling sausages and forming links.

● 13

Sauces and Purées the Easy Way

The KitchenAid® Fruit/Vegetable Strainer works with the Food Grinder to turn out silky applesauce, healthy homemade baby food, perfect raspberry coulis and much more. It purées any soft fruit or cooked vegetable and gets rid of seeds and skins. And it does all the work without straining your arm or staining your strainer!

Before processing fruits with tough thick skin (like oranges or grapefruits) remove the skin; also remove any large pits (like peach pits). Hulls and stems (including strawberry hulls and tomato stems) must also be removed. Vegetables and firm fruits must be cooked before processing.

If liquid collects in the hopper while you are straining high moisture foods such as tomatoes,

---

USE GRAPE CAUTION!

Slip-skin type grapes (the Labruscan family), including Concords, Catawba and Ontario grapes should NOT be processed in the Fruit/Vegetable Strainer. Damage to the attachment or the mixer could result. Only grapes from the Ninifera family, including Tokay and Thompson seedless may be processed.

---

do not add additional food. Keep the mixer running until residual moisture drains. Consult the instruction book for details.

Prepare for Pulp

In addition to placing the mixing bowl under the spout to catch puréed fruit or juice, you'll need another bowl to catch the pulp that comes out of the center of the strainer housing. You can adjust the texture of the finished product with this pulp. For example, when making Hummus (page 129) add the pulp back to the chickpea purée for a coarser texture. For Raspberry Coulis put the collected pulp back in the hopper and strain again. Discard the remaining pulp, which will consist mostly of raspberry seeds. For perfectly smooth baby food applesauce, discard all the collected pulp.

The Food Tray: Extra Room for Big Jobs

When you're putting up a summer's worth of tomatoes from the garden, add the Food Tray to the Fruit/Vegetable Strainer. It fits over the hopper of the Food Grinder so you spend less time reloading. It can also be used with the Food Grinder and Sausage Stuffer and is helpful when grinding large quantities of meat or stuffing sausages.

Raspberry Coulis

- **3   cups fresh raspberries**
- **1   tablespoon sugar (or more depending on sweetness of fruit)**
- **2   teaspoons lemon juice**

Assemble Food Grinder with Fruit/Vegetable Strainer and attach to stand mixer. Feed raspberries into hopper and collect raspberry purée in mixer bowl. Collect pulp in another bowl. Return pulp to hopper and strain again into mixer bowl. Stir in sugar and lemon juice until dissolved. Discard remaining pulp.

Make the Citrus Juicer Your Main Squeeze

 Got a lemon? Make lemonade the easy way with the KitchenAid® Citrus Juicer attachment. You'll get the last drop of juice from lemons, limes, oranges and grapefruit with a simple twist of the wrist. The juicer has a strainer, too, so seeds and bitter pulp are eliminated.

Once the juicer is attached, place a glass or pitcher under the spout to catch the juice. For small quantities, it may help to prop the glass up closer to the spout on an inverted bowl. Hold the fruit firmly and bring it in contact with the spinning reamer on the juicer. You'll have fresh, pure strained juice in a matter of seconds. Plastic parts of the juicer (everything except the aluminum shaft) are top-rack dishwasher safe to save clean-up time.

Turn Grain into Flour and Taste the Difference Freshness Makes

Grinding wheat, rice, corn, hulled oats or barley is as easy as attaching the Grain Mill to your KitchenAid stand mixer. Fresh flour has a nutty almost sweet flavor that's unmatched by commercially ground product. Wheat flour you mill yourself contains the entire nutritious kernel, including the bran and germ. Consult the instruction book for information on individual grains.

> **GRAIN MILL NO-NOS**
> Do not grind grains or nuts that are oily, or those that have a high moisture content, in your Grain MIll. For example, attempting to grind coffee beans, peanuts, sunflower seeds, soybeans or the like could damage the grinding mechanism.

How Many Wheat Berries in One Cup of Flour?

To make wheat flour you will be milling wheat berries, which are whole unprocessed kernels of wheat. One cup of wheat berries yields about 1½ cups of flour. Yields can vary depending on the variety of wheat and when it was harvested among other things. It's best to grind a bit more wheat than you think you will need and store the rest of the flour in an airtight container. Keep it in the refrigerator or freezer, since it is quite perishable.

Wheat berries can be purchased in natural food stores, usually in the bulk section, or ordered online. Hard red winter wheat is the most common variety and is perfect for breads and the other recipes in this book. Soft spring wheat is best used for cakes and cookies. The all-purpose flour sold in sacks in the supermarket is usually a mix of the two types.

Rise and Shine

Start the day with the recipes in this chapter and turn anyone into a morning person. Your KitchenAid® stand mixer makes quick work of coffee cake, biscuits, scones and quiche. With the Citrus Juicer attachment you can create custom juice blends in record time. Try wowing the brunch bunch with Mimosa Citrus Punch.

Of course, a healthy breakfast is just as important as a tasty one. With the KitchenAid® Grain Mill you can easily grind wheat berries into whole grain flour. You'll be amazed at the sweetness and depth of flavor freshly ground wheat brings to simple morning favorites like Whole Wheat Pancakes. Why not prepare Herbed Chicken & Apple Sausage to go with them using the Grinder and Sausage Stuffer? When you use only the best ingredients, sausage can be wholesome as well as incredibly delicious.

Having a great day is guaranteed when you start out with great food.

17

Whole Wheat Pancakes

2/3 **cup wheat berries*** *or* **1 cup whole wheat flour**

2 **teaspoons baking powder**

3/4 **cup whole milk**

1/4 **cup whole milk Greek yogurt**

3 **tablespoons vegetable oil**

1 **tablespoon honey**

2 **eggs**

Melted butter

Raspberries, blueberries or strawberries (optional)

Maple syrup (optional)

*Hard red winter wheat kernels are available at natural food stores, usually in the bulk section.

1 Attach Grain Mill to stand mixer. Place wheat berries in hopper; process on fine grind into bowl. Measure 1 cup flour*; place in small bowl. Stir in baking powder.

2 Remove Grain Mill; attach flat beater. Combine milk, yogurt, oil and honey in mixer bowl. Add eggs and beat on low until mixed. Gradually add flour mixture, beating on low just until mixed.

3 Heat griddle or nonstick skillet over medium heat. Brush with melted butter. Drop batter by 1/4 cupfuls onto griddle; spread into circle with back of spoon. Cook about 2 minutes or until bubbles form around edges. Flip pancakes and cook 1 to 2 minutes or until firm and browned on both sides.

4 Serve with syrup and berries, if desired.

*Store leftover flour in the refrigerator or freezer for another use.

menu ideas

SUNDAY BREAKFAST

•

Pomegranate-Orange Juice, 29

Maple Sage Breakfast Sausage, 13

Whole Wheat Pancakes

Chile-Corn Quiche, 32

18

Herbed Chicken & Apple Sausages

- **MAKES ABOUT 3 POUNDS**

3 pounds boneless chicken thighs with skin, excess fat trimmed, cut into 2-inch strips

1¼ cups (about 3 ounces) chopped dried apples

⅓ cup finely chopped shallots

3 tablespoons frozen apple juice concentrate, thawed

1 tablespoon kosher salt *or* 2¾ teaspoons regular salt

¾ teaspoon freshly ground white or black pepper

1 teaspoon dried sage

1 teaspoon crumbled dried rosemary

½ teaspoon dried thyme

Sausage casings, soaked and drained*

See page 13 of the introduction for more information.

1 Spread chicken on baking sheet. Refrigerate or freeze until slightly firm.

2 Assemble Food Grinder with coarse grinding plate; attach to stand mixer. Grind chicken into mixer bowl. Add dried apples, shallots, apple juice concentrate, salt, pepper, sage, rosemary and thyme. Mix well. Cover with plastic wrap and refrigerate 2 hours or until well chilled. Remove and wash grinder.

3 Reassemble grinder with Sausage Stuffer; attach to mixer. Stuff casings with chicken mixture. Refrigerate sausages, uncovered, for at least 4 hours and up to 1 day to cure.

4 Grill, broil or pan-fry sausages until cooked through (165°F). Serve hot.

This breakfast sausage is equally delicious made into patties. After step 2, form mixture into 3-inch patties. Pan-fry until cooked through (165°F).

20

Cherry-Coconut-Cheese Coffee Cake

22

**MAKES 10 SERVINGS
(ONE 9-INCH CAKE)**

2½ **cups all-purpose flour**
¾ **cup sugar**
½ **teaspoon baking powder**
½ **teaspoon baking soda**
6 **ounces cream cheese,
   divided**
¾ **cup milk**
2 **tablespoons vegetable oil**
2 **eggs, divided**
1 **teaspoon vanilla**
½ **cup flaked coconut**
¾ **cup cherry preserves**
2 **tablespoons butter**

1 Preheat oven to 350°F. Grease and flour 9-inch springform pan. Attach flat beater to stand mixer. Combine flour and sugar in mixer bowl. Reserve ½ cup flour mixture; set aside. Stir baking powder and baking soda into remaining flour mixture. Cut in 3 ounces of cream cheese on low until mixture resembles coarse crumbs.

2 Combine milk, oil and 1 egg in medium bowl. Add to mixer bowl; stir just until moistened. Spread batter on bottom and 1 inch up side of prepared pan.

3 Whisk remaining 3 ounces of cream cheese, remaining egg and vanilla in small bowl until smooth. Pour over batter, spreading to within 1 inch of edge. Sprinkle with coconut. Spoon preserves evenly over coconut.

4 Cut butter into reserved flour mixture with pastry blender or two knives until mixture resembles coarse crumbs. Sprinkle over preserves.

5 Bake 55 to 60 minutes or until golden brown and toothpick inserted into crust comes out clean. Cool in pan on wire rack 15 minutes. Remove side of pan; serve warm.

Mimosa Citrus Punch

- **10 medium oranges, divided**
- **8 limes, divided**
- **1 pint strawberries, stemmed and halved**
- **1 cup raspberries**
- **1 lemon, cut into ⅛-inch slices**
- **3 medium grapefruit**
- **½ cup light corn syrup**
- **1 bottle (750 mL) sparkling wine or ginger ale**
- **Fresh mint sprigs (optional)**

1 Separate 4 oranges into sections and slice 2 limes into ⅛-inch slices. Spread orange sections, lime slices, strawberries, raspberries and lemon slices on baking sheet. Freeze 4 hours or until firm.

2 Meanwhile, attach Citrus Juicer to stand mixer. Juice remaining 6 oranges, 6 limes and grapefruit into 2-quart pitcher. Add corn syrup; stir until dissolved. Refrigerate 2 hours or until cold. Stir in sparkling wine just before serving.

3 Place frozen fruit in glasses or punch bowl; fill with punch. Garnish with mint sprigs.

24

Berry Bran Muffins

1 Preheat oven to 350°F. Grease 12 standard (2 1/2-inch) muffin cups or line with paper baking cups.

2 Mix cereal and milk in bowl of stand mixer. Let stand 5 minutes to soften. Attach flat beater; add brown sugar, oil, egg and vanilla and beat until well blended. Combine flour, baking powder and salt in medium bowl. Add to mixer bowl; stir just until moistened. Gently fold in berries. Fill prepared muffin cups almost full.

3 Bake 20 to 25 minutes (25 to 30 minutes if using frozen berries) or until toothpick inserted into centers comes out clean. Cool in pan on wire rack 5 minutes; serve warm.

2	**cups dry bran cereal**
1 1/4	**cups milk**
1/2	**cup packed brown sugar**
1/4	**cup vegetable oil**
1	**egg, lightly beaten**
1	**teaspoon vanilla**
1 1/4	**cups all-purpose flour**
1	**tablespoon baking powder**
1/4	**teaspoon salt**
1	**cup fresh or frozen blueberries**

25

Tuscan Brunch Torta

- **MAKES 12 SERVINGS**

3	cups all-purpose flour
3/4	teaspoon salt
1	cup (2 sticks) cold unsalted butter, cut into pieces
6	to 8 tablespoons ice water
1	egg, separated
4	whole eggs
1	container (15 ounces) ricotta cheese
1	package (10 ounces) frozen chopped spinach, thawed and squeezed dry
1/2	cup freshly grated Parmesan cheese
1/2	teaspoon red pepper flakes
1/8	teaspoon ground nutmeg
8	ounces sliced prosciutto or smoked ham
1/2	cup Pesto Sauce (page 76)
1	jar (7 ounces) roasted red peppers, rinsed, drained and patted dry
4	ounces sliced provolone cheese
1	tablespoon milk

1 Attach flat beater to stand mixer. Combine flour and salt in mixer bowl; cut in butter on low until mixture resembles coarse crumbs. Add water, 1 tablespoon at a time, until dough forms a soft ball.

2 Shape two thirds of dough into disk; shape one third of dough into another disk. Wrap separately in plastic wrap; refrigerate 30 minutes or until firm enough to roll out.

3 Preheat oven to 375°F. Roll out large disk of dough into 13-inch circle on floured surface. Transfer to 10-inch deep dish pie plate; trim to 1/4 inch beyond rim.

4 Pierce dough all over with fork. Beat egg white; brush lightly over dough. Bake 10 minutes; cool on wire rack.

5 Beat 4 whole eggs on low speed in mixer bowl. Add ricotta cheese, spinach, Parmesan cheese, red pepper flakes and nutmeg; mix well. Layer half of prosciutto over cooled crust; spread spinach mixture over prosciutto. Layer remaining prosciutto, pesto, roasted red peppers and provolone cheese over top.

6 Roll out remaining dough to 12-inch circle. Place over filling; trim to 1/2 inch beyond rim and flute edge. Reroll pastry scraps; cut into decorative shapes and place over pastry. Cut several slits to allow steam to escape.

7 Beat remaining egg yolk and milk in small bowl; brush evenly over pastry. Place pie plate on baking sheet; bake 1 hour or until golden brown. Let cool on wire rack 15 minutes. Serve warm.

Walnut-Ginger Scones

1 cup toasted walnuts*
1 cup all-purpose flour
1 cup whole wheat flour
3/4 cup diced crystallized ginger
1/2 cup raisins
1/4 cup plus 1 teaspoon sugar, divided
1 tablespoon baking powder
1/2 teaspoon salt
1/2 teaspoon ground cinnamon
1/2 cup (1 stick) cold unsalted butter, cut into small pieces
3/4 to 1 cup half-and-half

*To toast walnuts, spread in single layer on baking sheet. Bake in preheated 350°F oven 8 to 10 minutes or until golden brown, stirring frequently.

1 Preheat oven to 425°F. Line baking sheet with parchment paper or grease well.

2 Assemble Rotor Slicer/Shredder with coarse shredding cone; attach to stand mixer. Shred walnuts into mixer bowl.

3 Remove Slicer/Shredder; attach flat beater. Add flours, ginger, raisins, 1/4 cup sugar, baking powder, salt and cinnamon to mixer bowl; stir until evenly mixed. Cut in butter on low until mixture resembles coarse crumbs. Add half-and-half by 1/4 cupfuls, mixing gently until dough comes together.

4 Pat dough into 10-inch circle on prepared baking sheet. Sprinkle with remaining 1 teaspoon sugar. Cut circle into 10 wedges. Pull wedges apart, leaving 1 inch between wedges.

5 Bake 15 minutes or until scones are golden brown. Cool on baking sheet 10 minutes. Remove to wire rack; cool completely.

28

Pomegranate-Orange Juice

1 Attach Citrus Juicer to stand mixer. Juice oranges into pitcher. Stir in pomegranate juice and cranberry juice.

2 Refrigerate 30 minutes or until cold. Stir in club soda just before serving. Garnish with orange slices, if desired.

4 oranges
3 cups pomegranate juice
1 cup cranberry juice
2 cups cold club soda
   Orange slices for garnish
   (optional)

Jelly Doughnut Bites

$^1/_2$ **cup plus 3 tablespoons warm milk (95° to 105°F), divided**
1 **package ($^1/_4$ ounce) active dry yeast**
$^1/_3$ **cup granulated sugar**
1 **tablespoon butter, softened**
$2^1/_2$ **cups all-purpose flour**
1 **egg**
$^1/_2$ **teaspoon salt**
$^1/_2$ **cup raspberry jam**
Powdered sugar

tip

These doughnuts are best eaten the same day they are made. They can be served warm or at room temperature. To rewarm, microwave on HIGH 10 seconds just before serving.

1 Combine 3 tablespoons warm milk and yeast in bowl of stand mixer. Let stand 5 minutes until bubbly. Attach dough hook to mixer. Stir granulated sugar, butter and remaining $^1/_2$ cup milk into bowl. Add flour, egg and salt; beat on medium until dough forms and cleans side of bowl. Add additional flour 1 tablespoon at a time if needed.

2 Shape dough into a ball. Place in large lightly greased bowl; turn once to grease surface. Cover and let rise in warm place 1 hour.

3 Grease 48 mini ($1^3/_4$-inch) muffin cups. Punch down dough. Shape pieces of dough into 1-inch balls; place in prepared muffin cups. Cover and let rise 1 hour. Preheat oven to 375°F.

4 Bake 10 to 12 minutes or until light golden brown. Remove to wire racks to cool.

5 Place jam in pastry bag fitted with small round tip. Insert tip into side of each doughnut; squeeze about 1 teaspoon jam into each center. Sprinkle with powdered sugar.

Chile-Corn Quiche

Pie Pastry for One-Crust Pie (page 182)

4 ounces Monterey Jack cheese, partially frozen

1 cup corn

1 can (4 ounces) diced mild green chiles, drained

¼ cup thinly sliced green onions

1½ cups half-and-half

3 eggs

½ teaspoon salt

½ teaspoon ground cumin

1 Prepare pastry. Preheat oven to 450°F. Line crust with foil; fill with dried beans or rice. Bake 10 minutes. Remove foil and beans. Bake 5 minutes or until lightly browned. Cool on wire rack. Reduce oven temperature to 375°F.

2 Assemble Rotor Slicer/Shredder with fine shredding cone; attach to stand mixer. Shred cheese into small bowl.

3 Combine corn, chiles and green onions in small bowl. Spoon into crust; top with cheese. Whisk half-and-half, eggs, salt and cumin in medium bowl. Pour over cheese.

4 Bake 35 to 45 minutes or until filling is puffed and knife inserted into center comes out clean. Let stand 10 minutes before serving.

32

Sweet Potato Biscuits

1 Preheat oven to 425°F.

2 Attach flat beater to stand mixer. Combine flour, brown sugar, baking powder, salt, cinnamon, ginger and allspice in mixer bowl. Cut in shortening on low until mixture resembles coarse crumbs. Stir in pecans.

3 Combine sweet potatoes and milk in small bowl; whisk until smooth. Stir into flour mixture until soft dough forms.

4 Turn out dough onto lightly floured surface; knead lightly. Roll ½ inch thick. Cut dough with floured 2½-inch round cutter. Place on ungreased baking sheet.

5 Bake 12 to 14 minutes or until golden brown. Serve warm.

2½ **cups all-purpose flour**
¼ **cup packed brown sugar**
1 **tablespoon baking powder**
¾ **teaspoon salt**
¾ **teaspoon ground cinnamon**
¼ **teaspoon ground ginger**
¼ **teaspoon ground allspice**
½ **cup cold shortening**
½ **cup chopped pecans**
¾ **cup mashed cooked sweet potatoes**
½ **cup milk**

33

For pumpkin biscuits, substitute ³/₄ cup canned pumpkin for the sweet potatoes.

Cinnamon-Date Scones

MAKES 12 SCONES

2 cups all-purpose flour
2 tablespoons granulated sugar
2½ teaspoons baking powder
½ teaspoon salt
½ teaspoon ground cinnamon
5 tablespoons cold butter, cut into pieces
½ cup chopped pitted dates
2 eggs
⅓ cup half-and-half or milk
Coarse sugar

1 Preheat oven to 425°F. Attach flat beater to stand mixer. Combine flour, sugar, baking powder, salt and cinnamon in mixer bowl. Cut in butter on low until mixture resembles coarse crumbs. Stir in dates.

2 Whisk eggs in small bowl. Add half-and-half; whisk until well blended. Reserve 1 tablespoon egg mixture. Stir remaining egg mixture into flour mixture until dough clings together.

3 Turn out dough onto floured surface. Knead gently 10 times. Roll dough into 9×6-inch rectangle. Cut rectangle into six 3-inch squares. Cut each square diagonally in half. Place triangles 2 inches apart on ungreased baking sheet. Brush with reserved egg mixture; sprinkle with coarse sugar.

4 Bake 10 to 12 minutes or until golden brown. Immediately remove from baking sheet; cool on wire rack. Serve warm.

34

menu ideas

BRUNCH

•

Mimosa Citrus Punch, 24

Chicken & Apple Sausages, 20

Tuscan Brunch Torta, 26

Scalloped Potatoes with Ham, 59

Cinnamon-Date Scones

Cherry-Coconut-Cheese Coffee Cake, 22

Green Onion Cream Cheese Breakfast Biscuits

MAKES 8 BISCUITS

2 cups all-purpose flour

1 tablespoon baking powder

1 tablespoon sugar

³/₄ teaspoon salt

1 package (3 ounces) cream cheese, cut into pieces

¹/₄ cup cold shortening

¹/₂ cup finely chopped green onions

²/₃ cup milk

1 Preheat oven to 450°F.

2 Attach flat beater to stand mixer. Combine flour, baking powder, sugar and salt in mixer bowl. Cut in cream cheese and shortening on low until mixture resembles coarse crumbs. Stir in green onions. Add milk; stir until soft dough forms.

3 Turn out dough onto well-floured surface. Knead gently 10 to 12 times. Roll or pat dough to ¹/₂-inch thickness. Cut dough with floured 3-inch biscuit cutter. Place on ungreased baking sheet.

4 Bake 10 to 12 minutes or until golden brown. Serve warm.

36

Coffee Cake with Chocolate Streusel

1 Preheat oven to 350°F. Grease 8- or 9-inch round cake pan.

2 Attach flat beater to stand mixer. Combine flour, brown sugar, granulated sugar, baking powder, baking soda and salt in mixer bowl. Cut in butter on low until mixture resembles coarse crumbs. Place ½ cup flour mixture in small bowl for streusel; stir in chocolate chips and pecans. Set aside.

3 Combine milk, egg and vanilla in small bowl; mix well. Add to flour mixture in mixer bowl; beat 1 minute or until blended. Spread batter in prepared pan. Sprinkle streusel evenly over batter.

4 Bake 40 minutes or until toothpick inserted into center comes out clean. Cool in pan on wire rack 15 minutes; cut into wedges. Serve warm.

1⅓ **cups all-purpose flour**
½ **cup packed brown sugar**
¼ **cup granulated sugar**
½ **teaspoon baking powder**
¼ **teaspoon baking soda**
¼ **teaspoon salt**
6 **tablespoons butter, softened**
½ **cup semisweet chocolate chips**
¼ **cup chopped pecans, toasted**
½ **cup milk**
1 **egg**
1 **teaspoon vanilla**

• **37**

Entertaining Ideas

Whether you plan a formal dinner party months in advance or throw an impromptu get-together for cocktails and munchies, the recipes in this chapter make culinary success a sure thing. Break the ice with delicious (and gorgeous) Frozen Mango-Lime Margaritas. They're a cinch with your KitchenAid® Ice Cream Maker attachment. And forget the onion dip—make Sausage Stuffed Mushrooms or Crisp Fish Cakes instead. They're easy with the Food Grinder and finger food never tasted so good or looked so elegant.

There's no need to admit how easy it is to prepare company-perfect ravioli with the Ravioli Maker. Let them think you slaved for hours filling each one by hand. From lofty soufflés to rustic pâtés, with KitchenAid it's all within reach.

Shrimp & Chile Empanadas

4 ounces cream cheese, softened

¹/₂ cup (1 stick) butter, softened

¹/₄ cup freshly grated Parmesan cheese

¹/₂ teaspoon dried oregano

¹/₄ teaspoon black pepper

1 to 1¹/₄ cups all-purpose flour

Shrimp Filling (recipe follows)

1 Attach flat beater to stand mixer. Combine cream cheese, butter, Parmesan cheese, oregano and pepper in mixer bowl; mix on low until smooth. Add flour; mix until dough forms that cleans side of bowl. Shape dough into two balls; wrap in plastic wrap and refrigerate 30 minutes or until firm. Prepare Shrimp Filling; refrigerate.

2 Place one ball of dough on lightly floured surface and flatten slightly. Knead 5 minutes or until smooth and elastic.

3 Roll dough to ¹/₈-inch thickness. Cut out circles with 3-inch biscuit cutter. Gather scraps into ball; wrap with plastic wrap and refrigerate. Repeat with second ball of dough. Roll out reserved scraps to make about 36 rounds.

4 Preheat oven to 450°F. Place 1 teaspoon filling on each round. Fold in half; seal edges with fork. Place on ungreased baking sheets.

5 Bake 10 minutes or until golden brown. Cool slightly on wire rack; serve warm.

Shrimp Filling

8 ounces cooked peeled shrimp

1 can (4 ounces) diced mild green chiles, drained

¹/₄ cup freshly grated Parmesan cheese

2 green onions, chopped

3 to 4 tablespoons chopped fresh cilantro

Process ingredients in food processor until finely chopped.

Sausage Stuffed Mushrooms

MAKES 30 APPETIZERS

$^1/_2$ **pound pork shoulder, trimmed and cut into 2-inch strips**

30 **medium fresh mushrooms**

1 **slice white bread**

1 **tablespoon chopped fresh parsley**

$^3/_4$ **teaspoon salt**

$^1/_4$ **teaspoon dried sage**

$^1/_8$ **teaspoon black pepper**

4 **ounces mozzarella cheese, partially frozen**

1 Spread pork on baking sheet; refrigerate or freeze until slightly firm. Remove stems from mushrooms; set caps aside. Assemble Food Grinder with coarse grinding plate; attach to stand mixer. Grind stems and bread into separate bowls; set aside.

2 Grind pork into mixer bowl. Add parsley, salt, sage and pepper. Remove Food Grinder; attach flat beater. Mix on low 1 minute or until well combined.

3 Brown sausage mixture in medium skillet over medium heat; remove with slotted spoon, leaving fat in pan. Add mushroom stems to skillet and sauté 3 minutes. Remove from heat and set aside. Preheat oven to 450°F.

4 Assemble Rotor Slicer/ Shredder with fine shredding cone; attach to mixer. Shred cheese into bowl; add mushroom stems, bread crumbs and sausage.

5 Fill mushroom caps with sausage mixture; place on baking sheets. Bake 15 minutes or until heated through. Serve hot.

42

Baked Brie with Nut Crust

MAKES 8 SERVINGS •

1 Preheat oven to 350°F. Assemble Rotor Slicer/Shredder with coarse shredding cone; attach to stand mixer. Shred nuts into shallow dish or pie plate.

2 Combine egg and cream in another shallow dish; whisk until well blended.

3 Dip Brie into egg mixture, then into nut mixture, turning to coat all sides and pressing onto cheese.

4 Transfer Brie to baking sheet; spread jam over top. Bake 15 minutes or until cheese is warm and soft.

$1/3$ **cup pecans**
$1/3$ **cup almonds**
$1/3$ **cup walnuts**
  1 **egg**
  1 **tablespoon heavy cream**
  1 **wheel (8 ounces) Brie cheese**
  2 **tablespoons raspberry jam**

• **43**

Country Pâté with Pistachios

8 bacon slices

1 tablespoon unsalted butter

1/2 cup finely chopped shallots

1 clove garlic, minced

1 pound boneless pork shoulder, cut into 2-inch strips, chilled

8 ounces boneless veal shoulder, cut into 2-inch strips, chilled

8 ounces chicken livers, trimmed, chilled

6 ounces sliced fresh pork fatback,* cut into 2-inch strips, chilled

2 eggs, beaten

2 tablespoons Cognac or brandy

2 teaspoons kosher salt

1/2 teaspoon dried thyme

1/2 teaspoon freshly ground white pepper

1/8 teaspoon ground allspice

Pinch ground cloves

Pinch freshly grated nutmeg

1/2 cup coarsely chopped pistachios

4 bay leaves

Coarse mustard, tiny sour pickles (cornichons) and sliced crusty bread

See page 13 of the introduction for more information.

1 Preheat oven to 325°F. Rinse 8 1/2 × 4 1/2-inch loaf pan with cold water. Line bottom and short sides of pan with 6 bacon slices, overlapping ends in center of pan and letting ends hang over sides. Line each long side of pan with 1 bacon slice. (The water will help bacon adhere to pan.)

2 Melt butter in small skillet over medium heat. Add shallots and garlic; cook about 3 minutes or until tender but not browned, stirring often. Transfer to bowl of stand mixer and let cool.

3 Assemble Food Grinder with coarse grinding plate; attach to stand mixer. Grind pork, veal, livers and fatback into bowl with shallot mixture. Add eggs, Cognac, salt, thyme, pepper, allspice, cloves and nutmeg; mix well. Stir in pistachios. Transfer to prepared pan and smooth top. Fold bacon slices over to cover pâté mixture; arrange bay leaves on bacon. Fit top with rectangle of parchment paper; cover tightly with foil.

4 Place loaf pan in roasting pan. Add hot water to roasting pan to come 1/2 inch up sides of loaf pan. Bake 2 hours and 15 minutes or until meat thermometer inserted into center of pâté reads 165°F (pierce through foil).

5 Remove loaf pan from roasting pan. Pour out water. Uncover loaf pan and pour out excess liquid. Return loaf pan to roasting pan to catch drips. Fit a second pan on top of pâté and weight with heavy cans to press pâté. Let cool 1 hour. Transfer weighted pan to refrigerator and refrigerate 8 to 12 hours.

6 Unmold pâté. Wipe away congealed juices and discard bay leaves. Wrap pâté in plastic wrap and refrigerate until ready to serve, up to 2 days. Let stand at room temperature before serving. Slice and serve with mustard, pickles and bread.

Avocado Lime Ice Cream

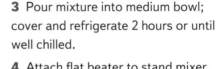

4 cups milk
1 cup sugar
3 egg yolks
4 ripe avocados
Juice and peel of 2 limes

1 Combine milk and sugar in medium saucepan. Cook and stir over medium-high heat just until bubbles begin to form around edge of pan. Do not boil. Remove from heat.

2 Whisk egg yolks in medium bowl. Gradually whisk in ³/₄ cup hot milk mixture. Slowly whisk egg mixture back into saucepan with remaining milk mixture. Cook over medium heat and whisk slowly until first bubble forms. Do not boil.

3 Pour mixture into medium bowl; cover and refrigerate 2 hours or until well chilled.

4 Attach flat beater to stand mixer. Cut avocados in half; remove pits. Scoop avocados into mixer bowl; add lime peel and juice. Beat on medium until smooth; scrape bowl. Add chilled milk mixture; beat on low until blended.*

5 Attach frozen Ice Cream Maker bowl and dasher to stand mixer. Turn mixer to stir; pour cold mixture into bowl with mixer running. Continue to stir 20 to 30 minutes or until consistency of soft-serve ice cream.

6 Transfer ice cream to airtight container and freeze several hours or until firm. Use within one week.

For a smoother ice cream, strain mixture through a fine-mesh sieve.

Chipotle Beer Fondue

1 Assemble Rotor Slicer/Shredder with coarse shredding cone; attach to stand mixer. Shred cheeses into mixer bowl. Add cornstarch; toss to coat.

2 Place beer and garlic in saucepan or fondue pot and bring to a boil over high heat. Reduce heat to low and slowly add cheese mixture, stirring constantly. Add chipotle peppers and green onions. Stir 2 to 3 minutes or until cheese is melted and mixture is smooth. Sprinkle with ground red pepper.

3 To serve, place fondue pot over low flame and serve with tortillas, French bread cubes, cauliflower florets, carrot slices or bell pepper slices. Use fondue forks or skewers for dipping.

8 ounces Swiss cheese, partially frozen

8 ounces Colby-Jack cheese, partially frozen

4 ounces Gouda cheese, partially frozen

1 tablespoon cornstarch

1 cup Mexican beer

1 clove garlic, minced

3 canned whole chipotle peppers in adobo sauce, minced

$\frac{1}{2}$ cup chopped green onions

$\frac{1}{8}$ teaspoon ground red pepper

Tortillas and/or French bread cubes

Cauliflower florets, carrot slices and/or bell pepper slices

47

Artichoke, Olive & Goat Cheese Pizza

● MAKES 2 PIZZAS

New York-Style Pizza Crust (recipe follows)

2 tablespoons olive oil

4 teaspoons minced fresh rosemary leaves *or* 2 teaspoons dried rosemary

6 cloves garlic, minced

1 cup (4 ounces) shredded Monterey Jack cheese*

1 cup water-packed artichoke hearts, sliced

8 oil-packed sun-dried tomatoes, drained and sliced (about 1 cup)

5 ounces soft goat cheese, sliced or crumbled

20 kalamata olives, pitted and halved (about ¹/₂ cup)

If desired, shred cheese with the coarse shredding cone of the Rotor Slicer/Shredder.

1 Prepare New York-Style Pizza Crust. Preheat oven to 500°F.

2 Brush olive oil over prepared crusts. Sprinkle with rosemary and garlic; brush again to coat with oil. Bake 3 to 4 minutes or until crust is light golden. Sprinkle each crust with ¹/₄ cup Monterey Jack cheese, leaving 1-inch border. Top with artichokes, tomatoes, goat cheese and olives. Sprinkle with remaining Monterey Jack cheese.

3 Bake 3 to 4 minutes or until crust is deep golden and cheese is melted.

New York-Style Pizza Crust

²/₃ cup warm water (110°F)

1 teaspoon sugar

1 teaspoon active dry yeast

1³/₄ cups all-purpose or bread flour

¹/₂ teaspoon salt

1 Combine water and sugar in small bowl; stir to dissolve sugar. Sprinkle yeast over water; stir. Let stand 5 to 10 minutes or until foamy.

2 Attach dough hook to stand mixer. Combine flour and salt in mixer bowl; stir in yeast mixture until soft dough forms. Knead on low 5 minutes or until dough is smooth and elastic, adding additional flour, 1 tablespoon at a time, if needed. Place dough in lightly greased medium bowl; turn once to grease surface. Cover and let rise in warm place 30 minutes or until doubled.

3 Punch down dough; knead on lightly floured surface 2 minutes or until smooth. Divide dough in half. Pat each half into flat disk. Let rest 2 to 3 minutes.

4 Pat and gently stretch each disk into 10-inch circle allowing it to rest for a few minutes if it becomes hard to stretch. Transfer to greased baking sheets or pizza peel. Proceed as recipe directs.

● **MAKES DOUGH FOR 2 THIN-CRUST PIZZAS (10 INCHES)**

Butternut Squash Ravioli with Sage Butter

**MAKES 4 SERVINGS
(ABOUT 4 DOZEN RAVIOLI)**

- 1 **small butternut squash, halved and seeded**
- 1 **tablespoon olive oil**
  Pinch salt and black pepper
- 1 **cup ricotta cheese**
- ¼ **cup grated Parmesan cheese**
- 1 **teaspoon freshly grated nutmeg**
- 1 **recipe Ravioli Dough (page 83)**
- 6 **tablespoons salted butter**
- 10 **fresh sage leaves, coarsely chopped, plus additional for garnish**
  Freshly grated Parmesan cheese

Ravioli make a great appetizer or first course. Plan on four to five ravioli per person.

1 Preheat oven to 400°F. Brush cut sides of squash with oil; sprinkle with salt and pepper. Place cut side down on baking sheet. Bake 45 minutes or until soft; let cool. Scoop out squash into medium bowl and mash (about 1 cup mashed squash). Stir in ricotta cheese, Parmesan cheese and nutmeg; set aside.

2 Meanwhile, prepare Ravioli Dough.

3 Attach Ravioli Maker to stand mixer. Fold one dough sheet in half. Fit folded end of dough between rollers and rotate handle one quarter turn just until rollers catch dough. Open loose ends of dough and drape over sides of Ravioli Maker.

4 Fit hopper into Ravioli Maker. Spread one spoonful of filling into hopper. Slowly turn handle, adding filling as needed. Place finished sheet of ravioli on clean cloth to dry 10 minutes. Repeat with remaining dough and filling.

5 Gently separate ravioli and trim edges. Keep ravioli in single layer to prevent sticking.* Bring large pot of salted water to a boil. Add ravioli; cook 2 to 4 minutes or until barely tender. Remove with slotted spoon; keep warm.

6 For sauce, melt butter in large skillet over medium heat. Add sage. Cook until butter begins to brown. Pour sauce over ravioli on serving plates. Sprinkle with Parmesan and garnish with additional whole sage leaves, if desired.

*Ravioli may be frozen for later use. Spread in single layer on parchment-lined baking sheet. Once frozen, transfer ravioli to freezer bags.

50

White Sangria

2 oranges, halved
2 lemons, halved
1/2 cup sugar
3 ripe peaches, pitted and halved
2 bottles dry, fruity white wine (such as Pinot Grigio), chilled
1/2 cup peach schnapps
2 cups ice cubes

1 Assemble Rotor Slicer / Shredder with thick slicing cone; attach to stand mixer. Slice oranges and lemons into large bowl. Sprinkle with sugar; mash lightly until sugar dissolves and fruit begins to break down.

2 Slice peaches into bowl. Stir in wine and peach schnapps. Refrigerate at least 2 hours or overnight. Transfer sangria to punch bowl and add ice cubes just before serving.

54

menu ideas

COCKTAIL PARTY

•

White Sangria

Sausage Stuffed Mushrooms, 42

Baked Brie with Nut Crust, 43

Country Pâté with Pistachios, 44

Rosemary Wine Crackers, 112

Chocolate Macarons, 166

Frozen Mango-Lime Margaritas

1 Combine mangoes, lime juice, water and sugar in food processor; process until smooth. Refrigerate 30 minutes or until well chilled.

2 Attach frozen Ice Cream Maker bowl and dasher to stand mixer. Turn mixer to stir; pour cold mixture into bowl with mixer running. Stir 20 minutes or until slushy. Stir in tequila and triple sec.

3 Meanwhile, rub rim of margarita glasses with lime slices; dip in salt.

4 Pour mixture into prepared glasses. Garnish with lime slices.

3 large ripe mangoes, cubed
1 cup fresh lime juice (8 limes)
1 cup water
$\frac{1}{2}$ cup sugar
$\frac{3}{4}$ cup tequila
$\frac{1}{4}$ cup triple sec
  Lime slices
  Coarse salt

55

menu ideas

LATIN FIESTA

Frozen Mango-Lime Margaritas

Shrimp & Chile Empanadas, 40

Black Bean Flautas with Charred Tomatillo Salsa, 126

Tacos Dorados, 75

Avocado Lime Ice Cream, 46

Sopaipillas, 152

Pot Stickers

- **MAKES ABOUT 3 DOZEN**

        2   cups all-purpose flour
      3/4   cup plus 2 tablespoons
            boiling water
      1/2   cup very finely chopped
            napa cabbage
        8   ounces lean ground pork
        2   tablespoons finely chopped
            water chestnuts
        1   green onion, finely chopped
    1 1/2   teaspoons cornstarch
    1 1/2   teaspoons dry sherry
    1 1/2   teaspoons soy sauce
      1/2   teaspoon minced fresh
            ginger
      1/2   teaspoon dark sesame oil
      1/4   teaspoon sugar
        2   tablespoons vegetable oil,
            divided
      2/3   cup chicken broth, divided
            Soy sauce or Ginger
            Dipping Sauce (page 52)

tip

Dumplings may be refrigerated for up to 4 hours or frozen for longer storage. Freeze in single layer; transfer to large freezer food storage bags. Do not thaw before cooking.

1 Attach flat beater to stand mixer. Place flour in mixer bowl. Pour in boiling water; stir until dough forms. Replace flat beater with dough hook; knead on low 3 minutes or until dough is smooth and satiny. Cover dough; let rest 30 minutes.

2 For filling, squeeze cabbage to remove as much moisture as possible; place in large bowl. Add pork, water chestnuts, green onion, cornstarch, sherry, soy sauce, ginger, sesame oil and sugar; mix well.

3 Divide dough into two equal portions; cover one portion with plastic wrap or clean towel while working with other portion. Roll out dough on lightly floured surface to 1/8-inch thickness. Cut out 3-inch circles with round cookie cutter. Place 1 rounded teaspoon filling in center of each dough circle.

4 Moisten edges of each dough circle with water; fold in half. Pinch edges together to make pleats. Keep finished dumplings covered while shaping remaining dumplings.

5 Heat 1 tablespoon vegetable oil in large nonstick skillet over medium heat. Place half of pot stickers in skillet, seam side up. Cook 5 to 6 minutes or until bottoms are golden brown.

6 Pour in 1/3 cup broth; cover tightly. Reduce heat to low. Simmer 10 minutes or until all liquid is absorbed. Repeat with remaining vegetable oil, dumplings and broth.

7 Serve with soy sauce or Ginger Dipping Sauce.

Cheese Soufflé

- **MAKES 4 SERVINGS**

4 ounces Cheddar cheese, partially frozen
¼ cup (½ stick) butter
¼ cup all-purpose flour
1½ cups milk, at room temperature
¼ teaspoon salt
¼ teaspoon ground red pepper
⅛ teaspoon black pepper
6 eggs, separated
Pinch cream of tartar (optional)

1 Preheat oven to 375°F. Grease four individual 2-cup soufflé dishes or one 2-quart soufflé dish.

2 Assemble Rotor Slicer/Shredder with coarse shredding cone; attach to stand mixer. Shred cheese into small bowl; set aside.

3 Melt butter in large saucepan over medium-low heat. Add flour; whisk 2 minutes or until mixture just begins to color. Gradually whisk in milk. Add salt, red pepper and black pepper. Whisk until mixture comes to a boil and thickens. Remove from heat. Stir in egg yolks, one at a time, and cheese.

4 Remove Rotor Slicer/Shredder and attach wire whip. Place egg whites in clean mixer bowl with cream of tartar. Whip on high until stiff peaks form.

5 Gently fold egg whites into cheese mixture until almost combined. (Some streaks of white should remain.) Transfer mixture to prepared dishes.

6 Bake about 20 minutes for individual soufflés (30 to 40 minutes for larger soufflé) or until puffed and browned and wooden skewer inserted into center comes out moist but clean. Serve immediately.

Scalloped Potatoes with Ham

1 Assemble Rotor Slicer/Shredder with coarse shredding cone; attach to stand mixer. Shred cheese into medium bowl; set aside.

2 Melt butter in medium saucepan over medium heat; whisk in flour, salt and pepper. Cook 1 minute. Gradually whisk in cream and milk. Bring to a boil; remove from heat. Stir in 1 1/2 cups cheese in two or three batches until melted and smooth.

3 Preheat oven to 350°F. Grease 12×8-inch baking dish.

4 Peel potatoes. Replace shredding cone with thin slicing cone; slice potatoes into mixer bowl. Layer one third of potato, half of onion and one third of sauce in baking dish. Layer with one third of potato, remaining onion, ham and one third of sauce. Top with remaining one third of potato and sauce.

5 Cover with foil; bake 50 to 55 minutes or until potatoes are almost tender. Sprinkle with remaining cheese. Bake 10 to 15 minutes or until cheese is golden. Let stand 10 minutes before serving.

8 ounces Swiss cheese, partially frozen
2 tablespoons butter
1 tablespoon all-purpose flour
3/4 teaspoon salt
1/4 teaspoon black pepper
1 1/4 cups heavy cream
1 1/4 cups whole milk
1 1/2 pounds russet potatoes
1 medium onion, thinly sliced and separated into rings
1/2 pound sliced or cubed baked ham

59

tip

To prepare ahead, bake 50 minutes or until potatoes are tender. Cool, cover and refrigerate up to one day. To serve, sprinkle with cheese and bake 15 to 20 minutes in preheated 350°F oven or until heated through and cheese is lightly browned.

The Main Event

Dinner time can be a lot more interesting with a little help from your KitchenAid® stand mixer and attachments. Instead of ordinary burgers, use the Food Grinder and upgrade to Ultimate Grilled Burgers. The taste and texture difference from regular supermarket meat will amaze and delight you. When the crowd gathers at your place, impress them with homemade sausages. It's not as hard as you'd think with the Grinder and Sausage Stuffer.

And don't forget pizza, pasta and tacos! With the Pasta Roller, making fresh fettuccine is so much fun even the kids will want to help. Pizza dough comes together quickly with the dough hook, and tacos taste much more authentic with queso blanco cheese freshly grated in the Rotor Slicer/Shredder. It's easy to turn dinner into a special event.

Ultimate Grilled Burgers

MAKES 4 SERVINGS

1½ **pounds boneless beef chuck, excess fat trimmed, cut into 2-inch strips**

1½ **teaspoons kosher salt** *or* **1¼ teaspoons regular salt**

½ **teaspoon freshly ground black pepper**

Canola or olive oil

4 **hamburger buns, split**

Sliced tomatoes, lettuce leaves, raw onion rings and pickle slices

Assorted condiments, such as ketchup, mayonnaise and mustard

1 Spread beef strips on baking sheet. Refrigerate or freeze until firm.

2 Assemble Food Grinder with coarse grinding plate. Grind beef into medium bowl. Mix in salt and pepper with clean hands. Do not overmix. Shape into four 4-inch patties, making 1-inch wide shallow indentation in center of each patty to discourage shrinkage. Cover with plastic wrap. Prepare grill for direct cooking.

3 Lightly brush patties with oil. Grill, covered, over high heat 2½ minutes or until browned on bottom. Turn and grill 2½ minutes or until cooked through (160°F). If flare-ups occur, move burgers away from flames. Grill buns, cut sides down, 1 minute or until toasted.

4 Serve immediately with desired toppings and condiments.

menu ideas

SUMMER AFTERNOON

Ultimate Grilled Burgers

Kohlrabi & Carrot Slaw, 135

Exotic Veggie Chips, 124

Butterscotch Oatmeal Cookies, 160

Candy Bar Ice Cream, 146

62

Lamb, Feta & Sun-Dried Tomato Sausages

- **MAKES ABOUT 3 POUNDS (16 TO 20 SAUSAGE LINKS)**

2½ **pounds boneless lamb shoulder (see Note), trimmed and cut into 2-inch strips**

8 **ounces sliced fresh pork fatback,* cut into 2-inch pieces**

⅓ **cup drained and chopped oil-packed sun-dried tomatoes**

⅓ **cup finely chopped yellow onion**

2 **cloves garlic, minced**

2 **teaspoons dried mint or basil**

2½ **teaspoons kosher salt *or* 2¼ teaspoons regular salt**

¾ **teaspoon red pepper flakes**

3 **ounces feta cheese, cut into ¼-inch cubes (about ¾ cup)**

Sausage casings, soaked and drained*

*See page 13 of the introduction for more information.

1 Spread lamb and fatback on baking sheet. Refrigerate or freeze until slightly firm.

2 Assemble Food Grinder with coarse grinding plate; attach to stand mixer. Grind lamb and fatback into mixer bowl. Add sun-dried tomatoes, onion, garlic, mint, salt and pepper; mix well. Cover with plastic wrap and refrigerate 2 hours or until well chilled. Remove and wash grinder.

3 Meanwhile, freeze feta cheese in single layer 1 hour. Just before stuffing sausages, fold feta into lamb mixture.

4 Reassemble grinder with Sausage Stuffer; attach to mixer. Stuff casings with lamb mixture. Refrigerate sausages, uncovered, for at least 4 hours and up to 1 day to cure.

5 Grill broil, or pan-fry sausages until cooked through (160°F). Serve hot.

Note: Lamb shoulder used to be a common cut for stews, but now most of it is cut into chops. Order it from your supermarket butcher or look for it in the meat department of markets that specialize in Mediterranean cuisine.

Serve these sausages with Pita Bread (page 120) and Garlic Tahini Sauce (page 138).

Sesame Pork with Thai Cucumber Salad

● **MAKES 4 SERVINGS**

1 large or 2 small pork tenderloins (about 1¼ pounds total)

¼ cup soy sauce

2 cloves garlic, minced
  Thai Cucumber Salad (recipe follows)

3 tablespoons honey

2 tablespoons brown sugar

1 teaspoon minced fresh ginger

1 to 2 tablespoons toasted sesame seeds*

To toast sesame seeds, spread seeds in small skillet. Shake skillet over medium heat about 1 minute until seeds begin to pop and turn golden.

1 Place pork in large resealable food storage bag. Add soy sauce and garlic. Close bag securely; turn to coat. Marinate in refrigerator up to 2 hours. Meanwhile prepare Thai Cucumber Salad and refrigerate.

2 Preheat oven to 400°F. Drain pork; reserve 1 tablespoon marinade. Combine honey, brown sugar, ginger and reserved marinade in small bowl.

3 Place pork in shallow foil-lined roasting pan. Brush with half of honey mixture. Roast 10 minutes. Turn pork over; brush with remaining honey mixture and sprinkle with sesame seeds. Roast 10 minutes for small or 15 minutes for large tenderloin or until internal temperature reaches 145°F when tested with meat thermometer inserted into thickest part of pork.

4 Place pork on cutting board; tent with foil and let stand 5 minutes. Cut into ½-inch slices and serve with Thai Cucumber Salad.

Thai Cucumber Salad

1 large seedless cucumber *or* 2 medium regular cucumbers

1 small red onion, cut into wedges

¼ cup rice wine vinegar

2 tablespoons lime juice

1 heaping teaspoon sugar

2 tablespoons chopped fresh cilantro

2 tablespoons chopped unsalted peanuts

menu ideas

TRY THAI TONIGHT

●

Sesame Pork with Thai Cucumber Salad

Pot Stickers, 56, or Crisp Fish Cakes, 52, with Ginger Dipping Sauce, 52

Cooked jasmine rice

Hot green tea

1 Wash but do not peel cucumber. Assemble Rotor Slicer / Shredder with thin slicing cone; attach to stand mixer. Slice cucumber into medium bowl. (If using regular cucumbers, cut in half lengthwise and scoop out seeds before slicing.) Replace thin slicing cone with thick slicing cone. Slice onion into same bowl.

2 Combine vinegar, lime juice and sugar in small bowl; stir into cucumber mixture. Cover and refrigerate salad for at least 30 minutes. Stir in cilantro and top with peanuts before serving.

Grilled Pizza Margherita with Beer-Risen Crust

● **MAKES 4 SERVINGS**

3/4 cup beer

1 package (1/4 ounce) active dry yeast

2 tablespoons plus 2 teaspoons extra virgin olive oil, divided

1 3/4 cups all-purpose flour

1 teaspoon salt

1 1/2 pints grape tomatoes, halved

1 clove garlic, minced

1/4 teaspoon dried basil

1/8 teaspoon salt

1/8 teaspoon red pepper flakes

6 ounces fresh mozzarella, cut into 12 slices

10 fresh basil leaves, thinly sliced

1 Microwave beer in small microwavable bowl on HIGH 25 seconds. Stir in yeast and 2 teaspoons oil; let stand 5 minutes or until foamy.

2 Attach dough hook to stand mixer. Combine flour and salt in mixer bowl; add beer mixture and stir until dough cleans side of bowl. Knead on low 5 minutes or until smooth and elastic. Divide dough in half and form into balls. Dust with flour; place in separate medium bowls. Cover; let rise in warm place about 1 1/2 hours or until doubled.

3 Meanwhile, heat 1 tablespoon oil in medium nonstick skillet over medium-high heat. Add tomatoes, garlic, basil, salt and red pepper flakes; cook 3 to 4 minutes or until tomatoes are very soft, stirring occasionally. Remove from heat.

4 Preheat grill for direct cooking. Oil grid.

5 Gently stretch each piece of dough to 9-inch circle on lightly floured surface. Transfer to floured baking sheets. Brush tops with remaining 2 tablespoons oil. Cover; let stand 10 minutes.

6 Reduce grill to medium heat. Carefully flip dough rounds onto grid, oiled side down. Grill, uncovered, 3 minutes or until bottom is golden and well marked. Turn crusts; spread each with half of tomato mixture, leaving 1/2-inch border. Top with cheese; cover and grill 3 minutes or until cheese is melted and crust is golden brown. Transfer to cutting board; sprinkle evenly with basil. Serve immediately.

68

Koftas
(Lamb Meatballs in Spicy Gravy)

● **MAKES 6 SERVINGS**

2 teaspoons Garam Masala (recipe follows)

2 pounds lamb shoulder, trimmed and cut into 2-inch strips

2 cloves garlic

2 eggs

1¹/₂ cups finely chopped onions, divided

¹/₂ cup chopped fresh cilantro

1¹/₂ teaspoons salt, divided

1 teaspoon minced fresh ginger

24 whole blanched almonds

1 to 3 tablespoons vegetable oil

1 teaspoon ground coriander

1 teaspoon ground cumin

1 teaspoon chili powder

¹/₂ teaspoon ground turmeric

2 tomatoes, seeded and chopped

¹/₂ cup water

1 cup plain yogurt

1 Prepare Garam Masala. Spread lamb on baking sheet. Refrigerate or freeze until slightly firm. Assemble Food Grinder with fine grinding plate; attach to stand mixer. Grind lamb and garlic into mixer bowl.

2 Add eggs, ¹/₂ cup onion, cilantro, Garam Masala, ¹/₂ teaspoon salt and ginger to lamb; mix well. Refrigerate at least 1 hour or overnight.

3 Shape mixture into 24 ovals or balls; insert 1 almond into each meatball. Heat 1 tablespoon oil in large skillet over medium-high heat. Add half of meatballs; cook 8 minutes or until brown, turning frequently. Remove meatballs from skillet. Repeat with remaining meatballs, adding oil as needed.

4 Reduce heat to medium. Add remaining 1 cup onion. Cook and stir 6 to 8 minutes or until browned. Stir in remaining 1 teaspoon salt, coriander, cumin, chili powder and turmeric. Add tomatoes; cook 5 minutes or until tomatoes are tender.

5 Add water; bring mixture to a boil over high heat. Add meatballs. Reduce heat to medium-low. Simmer 15 minutes or until cooked through. Remove meatballs from skillet to serving platter; keep warm.

6 Remove skillet from heat; place yogurt in small bowl. Stir in several spoonfuls of hot mixture. Stir yogurt mixture back into sauce in skillet. Cook over medium-low heat until sauce thickens. Do not boil. Pour sauce over meatballs. Garnish as desired.

70

Garam Masala

  2 **teaspoons cumin seeds**
  2 **teaspoons whole black peppercorns**
1¹/₂ **teaspoons coriander seeds**
  1 **teaspoon whole fennel seeds**
 ³/₄ **teaspoon whole cloves**
 ¹/₂ **teaspoon cardamom seeds**
  1 **cinnamon stick, broken in pieces**

Preheat oven to 250°F. Combine all ingredients and spread on
baking sheet; bake 30 minutes, stirring occasionally. Grind warm
spices in spice mill or clean coffee grinder. Store in refrigerator
in tightly covered glass jar.

● **MAKES ABOUT 3 TABLESPOONS**

Note: Prepared garam masala can be found in the spice aisle of
large supermarkets or at specialty grocery stores.

Duck Breast with Cherry Sauce & Sweet Potato Pancakes

- **MAKES 4 SERVINGS**

CHERRY SAUCE
- 1/2 **cup dried cherries**
- 1 **cup dry red wine**
- 1 **cup sour cherry preserves**
- 1/4 **cup red wine vinegar**

SWEET POTATO PANCAKES
- 2 **sweet potatoes, peeled**
- 1 **russet potato, peeled**
- 1/2 **cup all-purpose flour**
- 1/3 **cup minced green onions**
- 2 **eggs, lightly beaten**
- 1/2 **teaspoon salt**
- 1/2 **teaspoon black pepper**
- 1/4 **teaspoon ground nutmeg**
  Oil for frying

DUCK
- 4 **boneless duck breasts (about 2 pounds)**

CHERRY SAUCE

1 Soak cherries in wine in small saucepan 15 minutes or until plump. Add cherry preserves and red wine vinegar. Simmer gently 10 minutes; keep warm until ready to serve.

SWEET POTATO PANCAKES

2 Assemble Rotor Slicer/Shredder with coarse shredding cone; attach to stand mixer. Shred potatoes into mixer bowl. Squeeze as much moisture as possible out of shredded potatoes in colander or strainer.

3 Return potatoes to bowl. Add flour, green onions, eggs, salt, pepper and nutmeg; mix until combined. Heat 1/4 inch of oil in large skillet over medium-high heat. Pat handfuls of potato mixture into cakes about 3 inches in diameter. Cook in batches without crowding pan 3 to 5 minutes per side until firm and browned. Keep warm.

DUCK

4 Place duck breast, skin side up, on cutting board. Cut crisscross lines through skin and fat layer only. Cook, skin side down, in large skillet over medium heat 5 minutes or until fat is rendered and skin is browned, pouring off excess fat as needed. Turn and cook 5 minutes or until browned but still pink in center. Slice and keep warm.

5 Arrange duck and sweet potato pancakes on serving dishes. Top with Cherry Sauce.

Venetian Chicken with Creamy Pesto Sauce

● **MAKES 6 TO 8 SERVINGS**

1 cup Pesto Sauce (recipe follows)

2 tablespoons olive oil

2 red or yellow bell peppers, cut into chunks

2 pounds boneless skinless chicken breasts or thighs, cut into 1-inch chunks

1 teaspoon salt

$^1/_2$ teaspoon black pepper

1 cup half-and-half

Hot cooked spaghetti

$^1/_2$ cup grated Asiago or Parmesan cheese

1 Prepare Pesto Sauce. Heat oil in large nonstick skillet over medium heat. Add bell pepper; cook and stir 3 minutes. Add chicken, salt and pepper; cook and stir 5 minutes.

2 Stir in pesto and half-and-half; cook, stirring occasionally, 3 minutes or until chicken is cooked through and bell pepper is tender (about 5 minutes for chicken thighs).

3 Serve over pasta; sprinkle with cheese.

Pesto Sauce

2 cups fresh basil leaves (about 4 ounces)

1 cup fresh parsley

6 cloves garlic

1 cup freshly grated Parmesan cheese

1 teaspoon salt

$^1/_2$ teaspoon black pepper

$^2/_3$ cup olive oil

1 Assemble Food Grinder with fine grinding plate; attach to stand mixer. Grind basil, parsley and garlic into mixer bowl. Add Parmesan cheese, salt and pepper.

2 Remove Food Grinder and attach wire whip. Whip on medium-high 1 minute. Stop and scrape bowl. With mixer on high, gradually add olive oil in a thin, steady stream, whipping until absorbed. Refrigerate or freeze leftover sauce.

● **MAKES ABOUT 1$^2/_3$ CUPS**

menu ideas

WEEKNIGHT GOURMET

Venetian Chicken with Creamy Pesto Sauce

Spinach Soufflé, 128

Rosemary Lager Focaccia, 118

Espresso Gelato, 150

76

Fettuccine with Pork & Porcini Ragù

• MAKES 4 TO 6 SERVINGS

1 ounce dried porcini mushrooms, rinsed

1 cup boiling water

3 tablespoons olive oil

1½ pounds meaty pork neck

1 medium onion, chopped

2 cloves garlic, minced

1 can (28 ounces) crushed tomatoes

½ cup dry white wine, such as Pinot Grigio

2 tablespoons tomato paste

1 tablespoon finely chopped fresh rosemary

¾ teaspoon salt

½ teaspoon freshly ground black pepper

1 recipe Semolina or Egg Pasta Dough (page 82), cut into fettuccine

Freshly grated Parmesan cheese

1 Combine mushrooms and boiling water in small bowl. Let stand about 20 minutes or until mushrooms soften. Remove mushrooms and coarsely chop; set aside. Strain soaking liquid through fine mesh strainer. Discard grit; reserve liquid.

2 Heat 2 tablespoons oil in Dutch oven or large skillet over medium-high heat. Add pork neck; cook 6 minutes or until browned, turning occasionally. Transfer to plate.

3 Add remaining 1 tablespoon oil to Dutch oven; reduce heat to medium. Add onion; sauté 5 minutes or until onion is translucent. Add garlic and cook 1 minute or until fragrant. Stir in tomatoes, wine, mushrooms, reserved soaking liquid, tomato paste, rosemary, salt and pepper. Bring to a boil over high heat, scraping up browned bits with wooden spoon. Return pork to Dutch oven; reduce heat to medium-low. Cover and simmer 1 hour and 45 minutes until meat is tender and falling off bones, stirring occasionally. Meanwhile, prepare pasta.

4 Transfer pork to cutting board, keeping sauce simmering. Let pork cool until easy to handle. Cut meat from bones and chop; discard bones. Return meat to sauce. Adjust seasonings.

5 Bring large pot of salted water to a boil. Add pasta and cook 2 minutes or until barely tender, stirring occasionally. Drain well. Serve sauce over pasta with Parmesan cheese.

Pasta Perfection

Be forewarned: Once you make your own pasta it's hard to go back to store-bought. Homemade has a luxurious texture and tender bite that makes investing the extra time worth it. And with KitchenAid® pasta attachments, kneading, rolling, cutting and filling feel more like fun than work.

Taste the difference fresh noodles make in hearty Beef & Sausage Lasagna. Or experiment with Basil Pasta Aglio e Olio by pressing basil leaves right into the noodles. It's easy with the Pasta Roller. Spinach pasta or whole wheat pasta can add a healthy spin and delicious difference to recipes.

With the Pasta Press attachment you can even make fresh, delicious macaroni or rigatoni in a matter of minutes. Pasta night will never be the same!

Basic Pasta Doughs

Egg Pasta Dough

3 eggs
2 tablespoons water
1 tablespoon extra virgin olive oil
2¼ cups all-purpose flour

Suggested Roller Settings

Setting	Uses
1 or 2	Kneading and thinning dough
3	Thick egg noodles
4 or 5	Lasagna noodles, fettuccine, spaghetti, ravioli
6 or 7	Tortellini, thin fettuccine, linguine
7 or 8	Angel hair (capellini)

1 Attach flat beater to stand mixer; beat eggs, water and oil in mixer bowl at low speed to combine. In three additions, add flour to make dough that clumps together. Stop mixer and press a few tablespoons of dough into small ball; dough should feel tacky, moist and pliable. If too wet, beat in flour, 1 tablespoon at a time. If too dry, beat in water, 1 tablespoon at a time. Gather dough into a ball.

2 Replace beater with dough hook. Knead on low 5 minutes or until dough is smooth and elastic. Shape dough into ball and wrap in plastic wrap; let rest at room temperature 20 minutes or refrigerate until ready to use.

3 Cut dough into quarters. Flatten one piece of dough; dust with flour. Rewrap remaining pieces to prevent drying out. Attach Pasta Sheet Roller to mixer and set to thickness setting 1. Turn mixer to medium speed; feed dough through rollers three or more times, folding and turning each time until smooth. If dough feels sticky, dust with flour. Change to setting 2 and feed dough sheet through rollers twice. Feed dough through once at settings 3 and 4; roll to suggested roller setting. Let dough sheets rest on floured surface 10 minutes. Replace roller with desired Pasta Cutter. Feed dough sheets through cutter.

Semolina Pasta Dough: Substitute 1¼ cups semolina flour and 1 cup all-purpose flour for the 2¼ cups all-purpose flour.

● **MAKES ABOUT 1 POUND**

Ravioli Dough

1 Attach flat beater to stand mixer. Combine all-purpose flour, semolina flour, eggs, olive oil and salt in mixer bowl; mix until dough comes together. Replace beater with dough hook; knead on low 2 to 3 minutes or until smooth and elastic. Wrap dough in plastic wrap; let rest 20 minutes or refrigerate until ready to use.

2 Cut dough into quarters. Flatten one piece of dough; dust with flour. Rewrap remaining pieces to prevent drying out. Attach Pasta Sheet Roller to mixer and set to thickness setting 1. Turn mixer to medium speed; feed dough through rollers three or more times, folding and turning each time until smooth. If dough feels sticky, dust with flour. Change to setting 2 and feed dough sheet through rollers twice making sure dough sheet is as wide as rollers.

3 Feed dough through once at settings 3, 4 and 5. Lay finished dough sheet on lightly floured surface. Repeat with remaining pieces of dough. (Let dough rest in single layer to prevent sticking.)

● **MAKES ABOUT 1 POUND**

1¼ cups all-purpose flour
¾ cup semolina flour
3 eggs
1 tablespoon extra virgin olive oil
1 teaspoon salt

83

Eggless Dough for Pasta Press

1 Attach flat beater to stand mixer. Combine all-purpose flour and semolina flour in mixer bowl. Gradually add water on low. Stop when rough dough forms. Dough should stick together when pressed with fingers, but should be fairly dry. Add additional water by teaspoonfuls if needed.

2 Assemble Pasta Press with desired pasta plate; attach to stand mixer. Feed walnut-size pieces of dough into hopper and extrude pasta to desired shape according to instruction book.

● **MAKES ABOUT 1 POUND**

1½ cups all-purpose flour
1½ cups semolina flour
¾ cup water

Basic Pasta Doughs

Spinach Pasta Dough

1 package (10 ounces) frozen
   chopped spinach, thawed

3 eggs

1 tablespoon extra virgin
   olive oil

2¼ cups all-purpose flour

1 Place spinach in bowl of food processor; pulse until very finely chopped. Place spinach in clean kitchen towel and wring to remove as much liquid as possible.

2 Attach flat beater to stand mixer. Place spinach, eggs and oil in mixer bowl; mix on low. Gradually beat in flour until dough clumps together. Dough should feel tacky, moist and pliable. If too wet, beat in additional flour 1 tablespoon at a time. If too dry, add water 1 tablespoon at a time. Gather dough into ball.

3 Replace flat beater with dough hook. Knead on low 5 minutes or until smooth and elastic. Wrap dough ball in plastic wrap; let stand at least 30 minutes at room temperature or refrigerate until ready to use.

4 Cut dough into quarters. Flatten one piece of dough; dust with flour. Rewrap remaining pieces to prevent drying out. Attach Pasta Sheet Roller to mixer and set to thickness setting 1. Turn mixer to medium speed; feed dough through rollers three or more times, folding and turning each time until smooth. If dough feels sticky, dust with flour. Change to setting 2 and feed dough sheet through rollers twice. Feed dough through once at settings 3 and 4; roll to suggested roller setting. Let dough sheets rest on floured surface 10 minutes. Replace roller with desired Pasta Cutter.* Feed dough sheets through cutter.

Do not use spinach pasta for fine or angel hair pasta since small bits of spinach make dough difficult to cut.

● **MAKES ABOUT 1¼ POUNDS**

84

Whole Wheat Pasta Dough

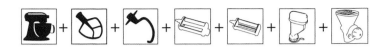

Attach Grain Mill to stand mixer. Place wheat berries in hopper and process on fine grind into bowl. Measure 3 cups flour and sift into mixer bowl. Remove Grain Mill; attach flat beater. Add egg mixture and salt to mixer bowl. Mix 30 seconds. Replace beater with dough hook; knead 1 to 2 minutes.

FOR PASTA PREPARED WITH ROLLER AND CUTTERS

Cut dough into eight pieces. Flatten one piece of dough; dust with flour. Rewrap remaining pieces to prevent drying out. Attach Pasta Sheet Roller to mixer and set to thickness setting 1. Turn mixer to medium speed; feed dough through rollers three or more times, folding and turning each time until smooth. If dough feels sticky, dust with flour. Change to setting 2 and feed dough sheet through rollers twice. Feed dough through once at settings 3 and 4; roll to suggested roller setting. Let dough sheets rest on floured surface 10 minutes. Replace roller with desired Pasta Cutter. Feed dough sheets through cutter.

FOR PASTA PREPARED WITH PASTA PRESS

Assemble Pasta Press with desired plate; attach to mixer. Feed walnut-sized pieces of dough into hopper and extrude pasta into desired shapes according to instruction book. Immediately separate pasta, dust with flour and spread in single layer on cloth or rack to dry 20 to 30 minutes.

● **MAKES ABOUT 1 POUND**

2 cups wheat berries *or* 3 cups whole wheat flour, sifted

2 eggs, beaten, plus water to equal ³/₄ cup

¹/₂ teaspoon salt

For best results, use the Fettuccine Cutter when preparing this pasta. Whole wheat dough has too coarse a texture to make angel hair or other fine pasta

When working with Pasta Press and whole wheat dough, pasta may be stiff and crumbly at first. If so, immediately squeeze extruded pasta into walnut-size pieces again and reuse it.

● 85

Spinach & Mushroom Cannelloni

MAKES 6 TO 8 SERVINGS

1 **recipe Egg Pasta Dough (page 82)**

18 **ounces fresh spinach***

2 **tablespoons olive oil**

8 **ounces cremini mushrooms, chopped**

1 **small onion, finely chopped**

1 **clove garlic, minced**

1 **cup whole milk ricotta**

½ **cup freshly grated Parmesan cheese**

1 **egg, beaten**

½ **teaspoon salt**

½ **teaspoon freshly ground black pepper**

¼ **teaspoon freshly grated nutmeg, divided**

3 **cups whole milk**

1 **dried bay leaf**

7 **tablespoons butter, divided, plus more for baking dish**

⅓ **cup all-purpose flour**

⅓ **cup freshly grated Parmesan cheese**

Shredded fresh basil

Two 10-ounce packages chopped frozen spinach, thawed and squeezed dry, can be substituted for the fresh spinach. Proceed to step 2.

1 Prepare pasta dough. For filling, rinse spinach and shake dry; place in large saucepan with water clinging to leaves. Cover; cook over medium heat 7 minutes or until wilted and tender, stirring occasionally. Drain; rinse under cold running water until cool. Squeeze all excess liquid from spinach a handful at a time. Chop spinach and place in large bowl.

2 Heat oil in large skillet over medium-high heat. Add mushrooms and cook 6 minutes or until they give off their liquid, stirring occasionally. Add onion and garlic; cook about 5 minutes until mushroom liquid is evaporated, stirring occasionally. Transfer to bowl with spinach and let cool. Stir in ricotta, Parmesan, eggs, salt, pepper and ⅛ teaspoon nutmeg.

3 For cream sauce, bring milk and bay leaf to a simmer in medium saucepan over medium heat. Melt 5 tablespoons butter in heavy medium saucepan over medium heat. Whisk in flour and reduce heat to medium-low. Let bubble without browning 1 minute. Whisk in hot milk with bay leaf. Bring to simmer, whisking often; simmer 5 minutes or until slightly thickened. Remove bay leaf. Add remaining ⅛ teaspoon nutmeg and season with salt and pepper. Dot top of sauce with remaining 1 tablespoon butter to prevent skin from forming.

4 Roll pasta dough to thickness setting 5. Cut into 5-inch squares and place in single layer on floured surface. Let rest 10 minutes.

5 Preheat oven to 350°F. Bring large pot of salted water to a boil. Add pasta squares and cook 2 minutes or until barely tender, stirring frequently to prevent sticking. Drain and transfer pasta to bowl of cold water to cool. Drain again. Place pasta squares on clean kitchen towels to remove excess water.

6 Spread about $1/2$ cup cream sauce in large buttered
baking dish. Place 1 pasta square on work surface; spoon
3 tablespoons filling along bottom edge and roll up from bottom.
Place seam side down in baking dish. Repeat with remaining
filling and pasta. Spread remaining sauce over pasta. Sprinkle
with Parmesan and dot with remaining 1 tablespoon butter.
(Cannelloni can be cooled, covered and refrigerated for up to
8 hours before baking.)

7 Bake about 25 minutes (35 minutes for chilled cannelloni)
or until sauce is bubbling and top is golden brown. Let stand
5 minutes before serving. Garnish with shredded basil.

Beef & Sausage Lasagna

● **MAKES 10 SERVINGS**

2 tablespoons olive oil

1 large yellow onion, chopped

2 cloves garlic, minced

1 pound ground beef

1 pound sweet Italian sausage, casings removed

1 can (28 ounces) crushed tomatoes

1 can (8 ounces) tomato sauce

1 can (6 ounces) tomato paste

1 cup hearty red wine, such as Chianti or Shiraz

$1/2$ cup water

1 teaspoon dried basil

1 teaspoon dried oregano

$1^1/4$ teaspoons salt, divided

$1/4$ teaspoon red pepper flakes

1 dried bay leaf

Olive oil

1 recipe Egg Pasta Dough or Semolina Pasta Dough (page 82)

1 container (32 ounces) ricotta cheese

1 cup freshly grated Parmesan cheese, divided

2 eggs, beaten

$1/4$ teaspoon freshly ground black pepper

4 cups (16 ounces) shredded mozzarella cheese

1 For sauce, heat oil in Dutch oven or large saucepan over medium-high heat. Add onion; sauté about 3 minutes or until softened, stirring occasionally. Add garlic; cook 1 minute or until fragrant. Add beef and sausage; cook about 10 minutes or until no longer pink, stirring to break up meat. Add tomatoes, tomato sauce, tomato paste, wine, water, basil, oregano, $3/4$ teaspoon salt, red pepper flakes and bay leaf; bring to simmer, scraping up browned bits in pan with spoon. Reduce heat to medium-low; simmer uncovered 1 hour or until reduced by about one fourth, stirring frequently. Remove bay leaf.

2 Prepare pasta dough. Cut pasta into 5×4-inch noodles. Arrange in single layer on kitchen towel; let rest 10 minutes.

3 Meanwhile, preheat oven to 350°F. Lightly oil 15×10-inch baking dish. Bring large pot of salted water to boil. Add lasagna noodles and cook 2 minutes or until barely tender, stirring frequently. Drain and transfer pasta to bowl of cold water to cool. Drain again and arrange in single layer on clean kitchen towels to remove excess water.

4 For filling, mix ricotta cheese, $1/2$ cup Parmesan cheese, eggs, remaining $1/2$ teaspoon salt and pepper in large bowl. Spread 1 cup sauce in baking dish. Layer with four lasagna noodles, slightly overlapping. Spread with one third of sauce, half of filling and 2 cups of mozzarella. Repeat with four more noodles, half of remaining sauce, remaining filling and 2 cups of mozzarella. Finish with four noodles and sauce and sprinkle with remaining $1/2$ cup Parmesan. Cover with oiled foil, oiled side down. (Lasagna can be cooled, covered and refrigerated for 1 day.)

5 Place dish on baking sheet. Bake 30 minutes. Uncover; bake 20 to 30 minutes more (30 to 40 minutes for chilled lasagna) or until sauce is bubbly. Let stand 15 minutes before serving.

Spinach Ravioli

- **MAKES 4 DOZEN RAVIOLI (ABOUT 4 SERVINGS)**

  - 1 recipe Ravioli Dough (page 83)
  - 1 package (10 ounces) frozen chopped spinach, thawed and squeezed dry
  - 2 cloves garlic, minced
  - ¼ teaspoon salt
  - ¼ teaspoon black pepper
  - ⅛ teaspoon ground nutmeg
  - ¾ cup ricotta cheese
  - ½ cup shredded Asiago or Parmesan cheese
  - 1 egg
  - 4 tablespoons (½ stick) butter, melted
  - 1 pint grape tomatoes, halved
  - Salt and freshly ground black pepper
  - Freshly grated Parmesan cheese

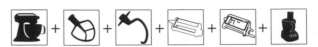

1 Prepare Ravioli Dough.

2 Combine spinach, garlic, salt, pepper and nutmeg in food processor; process until very finely chopped. Add ricotta cheese, Asiago cheese and egg; process until smooth. Refrigerate until ready to use.

3 Attach Ravioli Maker to stand mixer. Fold one dough sheet in half. Fit folded end of dough between rollers and rotate handle one quarter turn just until rollers catch dough. Open loose ends of dough and drape over sides of Ravioli Maker.

4 Fit hopper into Ravioli Maker. Spread a spoonful of filling into hopper. Slowly turn handle, adding more filling as needed. Place finished sheet of ravioli on clean cloth to dry at least 10 minutes. Repeat with remaining dough and filling.

5 Gently separate ravioli and trim edges. Keep ravioli in single layer to prevent sticking. Bring large pot of salted water to a boil. Add ravioli; cook 2 to 3 minutes or until barely tender. Remove with slotted spoon to serving dish; keep warm.

6 Gently stir in butter; season with salt and pepper. Toss with tomatoes and top with Parmesan.

menu ideas

GOURMET COOKING CLUB

·

Spinach Ravioli

Sausage Stuffed Mushrooms, 42

Artichoke, Olive & Goat Cheese Pizza, 48

Fettuccine with Pork & Porcini Ragù, 78

Creamy Lemon-Orange Gelato, 170

Basil Pasta Aglio e Olio

MAKES 4 TO 6 SERVINGS

PASTA
3^1/$_2$ **cups sifted all-purpose
     flour**
  4 **eggs**
  1 **tablespoon water**
^{1}/$_2$ **teaspoon salt**
  4 **ounces fresh basil leaves**

ROASTED GARLIC SAUCE
  2 **heads garlic**
  4 **tablespoons plus
     2 teaspoons olive oil**
     **Salt and coarsely ground
     black pepper**
  4 **teaspoons fresh lemon juice**
     Red pepper flakes

1 For pasta, combine flour, eggs, water and salt in bowl of stand mixer. Attach flat beater; mix until dough comes together. Remove beater and attach dough hook. Knead on low 3 to 5 minutes or until dough is smooth and elastic. Wrap dough in plastic wrap; let rest 20 minutes or refrigerate until ready to use.

2 Meanwhile, preheat oven to 350°F. Cut pointed tops off garlic heads; place on foil. Drizzle each with 1 teaspoon olive oil; sprinkle with salt and pepper. Wrap in foil; roast 30 minutes or until soft.

3 Cut dough into quarters. Flatten one piece of dough; dust with flour. Rewrap remaining pieces to prevent drying out. Attach Pasta Sheet Roller to mixer and set to thickness setting 1. Turn mixer to medium speed; feed dough through rollers three or more times, folding and turning each time until smooth. If dough feels sticky, dust with flour. Change to setting 2 and feed dough sheet through rollers twice.

4 Feed dough through once at settings 3 and 4. Lay dough sheet on lightly floured surface. Lightly dampen half of sheet with water. Arrange basil leaves on half of sheet; fold over other half to enclose leaves. Change rollers back to setting 3; feed folded sheet through rollers. Repeat at setting 4. Repeat steps with remaining dough pieces. Lay dough on lightly floured surface; let rest 10 minutes.

5 Replace roller attachment with Fettuccine Cutter. Feed dough sheets through cutter. Lightly flour fettuccine and arrange on floured surface in bunches.

6 Squeeze roasted garlic cloves into small bowl. Whisk in remaining 4 tablespoons olive oil, lemon juice and season with salt and pepper.

7 Meanwhile, bring large pot of salted water to a boil. Add pasta and cook 1 minute or until barely tender, stirring frequently. Do not overcook. Toss hot pasta with garlic sauce.

Tuscan Baked Rigatoni

1 recipe Eggless Dough
  for Pasta Press cut into
  rigatoni (page 83) *or*
  16 ounces dried rigatoni

1 pound bulk Italian sausage

2 cups (8 ounces) shredded
  fontina cheese*

2 tablespoons olive oil

2 bulbs fennel, thinly sliced

4 cloves garlic, minced

1 can (28 ounces) crushed
  tomatoes

1 cup whipping cream

1 teaspoon salt

1 teaspoon black pepper

8 cups packed torn stemmed
  spinach

1 can (about 15 ounces)
  cannellini beans, rinsed
  and drained

2 tablespoons pine nuts

$^1/_2$ cup grated Parmesan
  cheese

*If desired, shred cheese with
the coarse shredding cone of the
Rotor Slicer/Shredder.*

1 Prepare pasta with Pasta Press. Preheat oven to 350°F. Grease 4-quart casserole.

2 Brown sausage in large skillet over medium-high heat, stirring to break up meat; drain fat. Transfer sausage to large bowl. Add fontina cheese; mix well.

3 For sauce, heat oil in same skillet; add fennel and garlic. Cook and stir over medium heat 3 minutes or until fennel is tender. Add tomatoes, cream, salt and pepper; cook and stir until slightly thickened. Stir in spinach, beans and pine nuts; cook until heated through.

4 Bring large pot of salted water to a boil. Cook fresh rigatoni 2 to 3 minutes or dried rigatoni according to package directions until barely tender. Drain and add to sausage mixture. Pour sauce over pasta mixture; toss to coat. Transfer to prepared casserole; sprinkle evenly with Parmesan cheese. Bake 30 minutes or until bubbly and heated through.

94

Mac & Cheesiest

1 Prepare pasta with Pasta Press. Assemble Rotor Slicer/ Shredder with coarse shredding cone; attach to stand mixer. Shred Cheddar cheese into mixer bowl; reserve ½ cup. Shred Gouda, Gruyère and American cheeses into mixer bowl.

2 Preheat oven to 350°F. Melt butter in large saucepan or deep skillet over medium-low heat until bubbly. Whisk in flour until smooth paste forms; cook and stir 2 minutes without browning. Gradually whisk in milk over medium heat; cook 6 to 8 minutes, whisking constantly until mixture begins to bubble and thickens slightly. Add salt, nutmeg, black pepper and hot pepper sauce, if desired. Remove pan from heat and stir in cheeses until smooth.

3 Meanwhile, bring large pot of salted water to a boil. Cook fresh macaroni 2 minutes or dried macaroni according to package directions until barely tender, stirring frequently. Run under cold water to stop cooking; drain. Stir pasta into sauce. Transfer to 2-quart baking dish; sprinkle with reserved ½ cup Cheddar cheese. Bake 20 to 30 minutes or until golden brown.

- **1** **recipe Eggless Dough for Pasta Press cut into small macaroni (page 83)** *or* **8 ounces dried elbow macaroni**
- **8** **ounces Cheddar cheese, partially frozen**
- **3** **ounces aged Gouda cheese, partially frozen**
- **2** **ounces Gruyère or Swiss cheese, partially frozen**
- **2** **ounces American cheese, partially frozen**
- **4** **tablespoons butter**
- **5** **tablespoons flour**
- **2¾** **cups warm milk**
- **1** **teaspoon salt**
- **¼** **teaspoon ground nutmeg**
- **¼** **teaspoon ground black pepper**
- **2** **to 3 drops hot pepper sauce (optional)**

● 95

"Straw and Hay" with Asparagus & Prosciutto

MAKES 4 TO 6 SERVINGS

1/2 pound Egg Pasta Dough
(page 82), cut into wide or
extra-wide noodles
(see tip)

1/2 pound Spinach Pasta
Dough (page 84), cut
into wide or extra-wide
noodles (see tip)

1 pound thin asparagus,
stems trimmed

2 tablespoons unsalted
butter

1/2 cup minced yellow onion

4 ounces sliced prosciutto,
finely diced

1 1/3 cups heavy whipping cream

1/2 cup freshly grated
Parmesan cheese, plus
additional for serving

Salt and freshly ground
black pepper

1 Prepare Egg Pasta and Spinach Pasta.

2 Bring large pot of salted water to a boil. Cut asparagus crosswise into 1-inch pieces, separating asparagus tips from stems. Add stems to boiling water and cook 1 minute. Add tips and continue cooking until crisp-tender, about 3 minutes more. Remove asparagus with slotted spoon to bowl of cold water to stop cooking. Drain and set aside. Return water to a boil.

3 Melt butter in large skillet over medium heat. Add onion; sauté 3 minutes or until softened. Add prosciutto; sauté 3 minutes. Add cream; bring to a boil over high heat. Boil 3 minutes or until slightly reduced. Stir in asparagus. Reduce heat to very low and keep warm.

4 Add egg and spinach pasta to boiling water and cook 2 minutes or until barely tender, stirring frequently. Drain well; return to pot.

5 Add cream mixture and Parmesan to pasta; mix well. Season with salt and pepper. Serve hot with additional Parmesan, if desired.

(tip)

It's best to prepare a full recipe of both Egg Pasta and Spinach Pasta dough, cut them into noodles and freeze leftover noodles for another recipe.

Fettuccine with Vegetable Marinara Sauce

2 tablespoons extra virgin olive oil

1 medium yellow onion, finely chopped

1 small carrot, finely chopped

1 small stalk celery, finely chopped

2 cloves garlic, finely chopped

1 can (28 ounces) peeled plum tomatoes in juice

1/2 cup water

1/3 cup packed chopped fresh basil leaves

Salt and freshly ground black pepper

2 tablespoons butter, thinly sliced

1 recipe Egg Pasta Dough or Semolina Pasta Dough (page 82), cut into fettuccine

Freshly grated Parmesan cheese

1 Heat oil in large saucepan over medium heat. Add onion, carrot, celery and garlic. Cover and cook about 5 minutes or until onion is golden and tender, stirring occasionally.

2 Drain tomatoes, reserving juice. Coarsely crush tomatoes with fingers or wooden spoon. Add tomatoes, reserved juice and water to saucepan; bring to a boil over high heat. Reduce heat to medium-low. Simmer, uncovered, about 45 minutes or until slightly thickened and reduced, stirring frequently. Stir in basil during last 5 minutes of cooking. Season to taste with salt and pepper.

3 Meanwhile, prepare pasta. Bring large pot of salted water to a boil. Add pasta and cook 2 minutes or until barely tender, stirring frequently. Drain and return to pot. Add butter; toss gently until pasta is coated and butter melts. Serve sauce over pasta; top with Parmesan cheese.

98

Puttanesca with Angel Hair Pasta

1 recipe Egg Pasta Dough (page 82), cut into angel hair
2 tablespoons olive oil
2 to 3 anchovy filets, chopped
3 cloves garlic, minced
2 tablespoons tomato paste
2 cans (15 ounces each) diced tomatoes
1 teaspoon dried oregano
1 teaspoon dried basil
Salt and black pepper
1 can (14 ounces) tomato sauce
1/2 cup pitted Greek olives, coarsely chopped
2 tablespoons rinsed and drained capers
1/2 to 1 1/2 teaspoons red pepper flakes

1 Prepare pasta. Heat oil in large skillet over medium-low heat. Add anchovies; sauté 2 to 3 minutes. Add garlic; cook until lightly browned. Add tomato paste and cook 2 minutes.

2 Stir in tomatoes, oregano, basil, salt and pepper. Increase heat to medium; cook about 30 minutes or until mixture becomes saucy, stirring occasionally.

3 Turn heat to medium-low and add tomato sauce, olives, capers and red pepper flakes; simmer 10 minutes.

4 Meanwhile, bring large pot of salted water to a boil. Add pasta and cook 1 minute, stirring frequently. Drain; toss with sauce.

menu ideas

PASTA PARTY

Puttanesca with Angel Hair Pasta

"Straw and Hay" with Asparagus & Prosciutto, 96

Basil Pasta Aglio e Olio, 92

Chocolate Ravioli with White Chocolate Sauce, 164

100

The Bread Basket

Nothing creates a sense of home like the smell of freshly baked bread and nothing makes it easier than your KitchenAid® stand mixer. No need to knead until your back is sore—the trusty dough hook takes care of the hard work. Bring the world to your table with easy recipes for Pita Bread or Naan. No time for yeast bread? Try your hand at crackers, muffins, popovers or Brazilian Cheese Rolls.

With the Grain Mill attachment you can even grind your own wheat flour. You'll find that freshness really makes a difference in flavor. So make room in that bread basket for a new favorite—maybe it will be slightly sweet Anadama Bread or slightly spicy Jalapeño Corn Muffins, or maybe both. When it comes to bread, your KitchenAid stand mixer is always ready to rise to the occasion.

Anadama Bread

MAKES 2 LOAVES

2 cups water
$^1/_2$ cup yellow cornmeal
4 tablespoons butter, cut into pieces
$^1/_2$ cup molasses
$5^1/_2$ to 6 cups all-purpose flour, divided
1 package ($^1/_4$ ounce) active dry yeast
1 teaspoon salt

1 Bring water to a boil in medium saucepan. Whisk in cornmeal; cook 1 minute, whisking constantly. Reduce heat to low; whisk in butter. Cook 3 minutes, stirring frequently. Stir in molasses. Transfer mixture to bowl of stand mixer; let stand 15 to 20 minutes to cool.

2 Attach flat beater; stir in 2 cups flour, yeast and salt on low until rough dough forms. Replace beater with dough hook. Knead on low 5 to 7 minutes adding remaining flour $^1/_2$ cup at a time until dough is smooth and elastic (dough will be slightly sticky).

3 Shape dough into a ball. Place in large lightly greased bowl; turn once to grease surface. Cover; let rise in warm place about 1 hour or until doubled.

4 Punch down dough. Knead dough on well-floured surface 1 minute. Cut dough in half. Cover with towel; let rest 10 minutes.

5 Grease two 8-inch loaf pans. Shape dough into loaves and place in pans. Cover; let rise in warm place about 30 minutes or until doubled.

6 Preheat oven to 350°F. Bake 30 to 35 minutes or until loaves are browned and sound hollow when tapped. Immediately remove from pans; cool on wire racks.

Naan (Indian Flatbread)

● **MAKES 6 NAAN**

¹/₄ **cup plus 2 tablespoons warm water, divided**

1 **package (¹/₄ ounce) active dry yeast**

1 **teaspoon sugar**

3 **cups all-purpose flour**

1 **teaspoon salt**

1 **teaspoon kalonji* seeds or poppy seeds (optional)**

¹/₂ **cup plain whole milk Greek yogurt**

4 **tablespoons melted butter, plus additional butter or oil for brushing on naan**

*Kalonji seed is often called onion seed or black cumin seed. It is available in Indian markets and is traditional in some varieties of naan.

1 Place 2 tablespoons water in small bowl; stir in yeast and sugar. Let stand 10 minutes until foamy. Attach dough hook to stand mixer. Place flour, salt and kalonji, if desired, in mixer bowl; mix on low to combine.

2 Add yeast mixture, yogurt and 4 tablespoons butter; mix on low until combined. Add remaining ¹/₄ cup water by tablespoonfuls until dough comes together and cleans side of bowl. (You may not need all the water.) Knead on low 2 to 3 minutes or until dough is smooth and elastic.

3 Shape dough into a ball. Place in large lightly greased bowl; turn once to grease surface. Cover; let rise in warm place 1¹/₂ to 2 hours or until doubled.

4 Punch dough down; divide into six pieces. Roll into balls and place on greased plate. Cover; let rest 10 to 15 minutes.

5 Meanwhile, prepare grill for direct cooking or preheat oven to 500°F with baking stone on rack in lower third of oven. (Remove other racks.)

6 Place each ball of dough on lightly floured surface; roll and stretch into ¹/₈-inch-thick oval. Place 2 or 3 naan on grill or baking stone. Grill, covered, or bake 2 minutes until puffed. Turn, brush top with butter and grill or bake 1 to 2 minutes until browned in patches on both sides. Brush bottom with butter; serve warm with chutney, if desired.

Whole Wheat Popovers

MAKES 6 POPOVERS

1¼ **cups whole wheat pastry flour***

1¼ **cups milk**

3 **eggs**

2 **tablespoons melted butter**

¼ **teaspoon salt**

1 **tablespoon cold butter, cut into 6 pieces**

*Whole wheat pastry flour is available at natural food stores and some supermarkets.

Popovers are even better made from freshly ground wheat. Attach Grain Mill to stand mixer. Place about 1 cup wheat berries in hopper; process on fine grind into bowl. Sift flour and measure 1¼ cups.

1 Position rack in lower third of oven. Preheat oven to 400°F. Spray popover pan with nonstick cooking spray. (If popover pan is not available, jumbo muffin pans or custard cups may be used.)

2 Attach wire whip to stand mixer. Place flour, milk, eggs, melted butter and salt in mixer bowl; whip on medium until batter is smooth, scraping bowl occasionally.

3 Meanwhile, place popover pan in oven 2 minutes to preheat. Immediately place one piece of cold butter in each popover cup and return to oven 1 minute or until butter melts.

4 Fill each cup half full. Bake 25 minutes. Do not open oven or popovers may fall. Reduce oven temperature to 300°F. Bake 25 minutes more. Immediately invert onto wire rack. Serve warm.

108

Brazilian Cheese Rolls (Pão de Queijo)

1 Preheat oven to 350°F.

2 Combine milk, butter and oil in small saucepan. Bring to a boil over medium heat, stirring to melt butter. Once mixture reaches a boil, remove from heat.

3 Transfer mixture to bowl of stand mixer; attach flat beater. Beat in tapioca flour. (Mixture will be thick and stretchy.) Beat in eggs, one at a time. Beat in cheese. Mixture will be very stiff. Cool mixture in bowl until easy to handle.

4 Take heaping tablespoons of dough with floured hands and roll into golf-ball-size balls. Place on baking sheet about 1 inch apart.

5 Bake 20 to 25 minutes or until puffed and golden. Serve warm.

1 cup whole milk

$^1/_4$ cup (4 tablespoons) butter, cut into pieces

$^1/_4$ cup vegetable oil

2 cups plus 2 tablespoons tapioca flour*

2 eggs

1 cup grated Parmesan cheese or other firm cheese

*Sometimes labeled tapioca starch.

● **109**

Pretzel Rolls

MAKES 12 ROLLS

1¼ cups lager or nonalcoholic beer, at room temperature

3 tablespoons light brown sugar

2 tablespoons milk

2 tablespoons unsalted butter, melted

1 package (¼ ounce) rapid-rise active dry yeast

3 to 4 cups bread flour

2 teaspoons salt

4 quarts water

½ cup baking soda

2 teaspoons kosher salt

110

1 Attach flat beater to stand mixer. Place lager, brown sugar, milk, butter and yeast in mixer bowl. Stir in 1 cup flour and salt on low. Gradually stir in enough remaining flour to make stiff dough that cleans side of bowl. Replace beater with dough hook. Knead on low 8 minutes or until dough is smooth and slightly tacky, adding more flour as needed.

2 Shape dough into a ball. Place in large lightly greased bowl; turn once to grease surface. Cover; let rise in warm place 1 hour or until doubled.

3 Turn out dough onto lightly floured surface; knead 1 minute. Divide dough into 12 equal pieces. Shape each piece into ball. Smooth surface by pulling top of dough underneath and pinching bottom together. Place on ungreased baking sheet. Cover; let rise in warm place 30 minutes or until doubled.

4 Meanwhile, position oven rack in center of oven. Preheat oven to 425°F. Grease second baking sheet.

5 Bring water and baking soda to a boil in large pot. Add rolls to water in batches; cook until puffed, turning once. Drain rolls on clean kitchen towel. Place rolls 2 inches apart on prepared baking sheet. Cut 1½-inch X in top of each roll with kitchen shears. Sprinkle with kosher salt.

6 Bake 15 to 18 minutes or until browned. Remove to wire rack to cool.

Rosemary Wine Crackers

MAKES ABOUT 2 DOZEN CRACKERS

2/3 cup wheat berries *or* 1 cup whole wheat flour

1 tablespoon chopped fresh rosemary leaves

1/8 teaspoon salt

3 tablespoons olive oil

1/4 cup wine (preferably a fruity white or rosé)

Coarse salt (optional)

1 Attach Grain Mill to stand mixer. Place wheat berries in hopper and process on fine grind into bowl. Preheat oven to 400°F.

2 Measure 1 cup flour* into food processor; add rosemary and salt. With motor running, add olive oil and wine gradually through feed tube. When mixture becomes dough ball on top of blade, stop adding wine. Remove dough to cookie sheet lined with lightly floured parchment paper.

3 Roll dough as thin as possible (1/8 inch or less) on cookie sheet. Sprinkle with coarse salt, if desired, and roll lightly to press salt into dough. Score crackers into squares or diamonds with knife or pizza cutter.

4 Bake 10 to 15 minutes or until crackers begin to brown around edges, rotating cookie sheet halfway through baking time. Remove to wire rack to cool. Break into individual crackers. Store in airtight container. To recrisp, place crackers in 350°F oven for 5 minutes.

Store leftover flour in refrigerator or freezer for another use.

Variation: Making crackers is surprisingly easy. This recipe can easily be doubled or adjusted to suit personal tastes. Because crackers don't need to rise, whole wheat flour works well. You could also swap out some of the wheat flour for rye or buckwheat flour. Instead of wine, you could use fruit juice or even water.

112

Red Pepper Bread

**MAKES 20 SLICES
(1 LARGE LOAF OR 2 SMALL LOAVES)**

2 to 2½ cups all-purpose flour, divided

1 cup whole wheat flour

2 tablespoons grated Parmesan cheese

1 package (¼ ounce) rapid-rise active dry yeast

1 teaspoon dried rosemary, plus additional for sprinkling

½ teaspoon salt

¼ teaspoon dried thyme

1¼ cups hot water (130°F)

1 tablespoon olive or vegetable oil

½ cup chopped roasted red pepper

1 egg white, beaten

2 teaspoons water

1 Attach dough hook to stand mixer. Place 1 cup all-purpose flour, whole wheat flour, cheese, yeast, 1 teaspoon rosemary, salt and thyme in mixer bowl. Stir in hot water and oil on low until mixture is smooth; stir in red pepper. Stir in enough remaining all-purpose flour to form soft dough that cleans side of bowl.

2 Knead on low 2 to 3 minutes or until smooth and elastic, adding additional all-purpose flour, if necessary. Shape dough into a ball. Place in large lightly greased bowl; turn once to grease surface. Cover; let rise in warm place 30 minutes or until doubled.

3 Punch down dough; shape into one large or two small round loaves on greased baking sheet. Cover; let rise 30 minutes or until doubled.

4 Preheat oven to 375°F. Slash top of dough with sharp knife. Mix egg white and 2 teaspoons water in small cup; brush over dough and sprinkle with additional rosemary, if desired.

5 Bake 35 to 40 minutes for large loaf (25 to 30 minutes for small loaves) or until bread is golden and sounds hollow when gently tapped. Cool on wire rack.

Bacon-Jalapeño Corn Bread

MAKES 9 TO 12 SERVINGS

4 slices bacon
¹/₄ cup minced green onions
2 jalapeño peppers,* seeded and minced
1 cup all-purpose flour
1 cup yellow cornmeal
2¹/₂ teaspoons baking powder
³/₄ teaspoon salt
¹/₂ teaspoon baking soda
³/₄ cup plain yogurt
³/₄ cup milk
¹/₄ cup (¹/₂ stick) butter, melted
1 egg, lightly beaten
¹/₂ cup (2 ounces) shredded Cheddar cheese

*Jalapeño peppers can sting and irritate the skin, so wear rubber gloves when handling peppers and do not touch your eyes.

1 Preheat oven to 400°F.

2 Cook bacon in large skillet over medium heat until crisp. Drain on paper towels. Pour 2 tablespoons drippings into 9-inch square baking pan or cast iron skillet.

3 Crumble bacon into small bowl; add green onions and jalapeños. Attach flat beater to stand mixer. Combine flour, cornmeal, baking powder, salt and baking soda in mixer bowl.

4 Add yogurt, milk, butter and egg; mix on low just until moistened. Stir in bacon mixture. Pour into prepared pan; sprinkle with cheese.

5 Bake 20 to 25 minutes or until toothpick inserted into center comes out clean. Cut into squares or wedges.

116

Wild Rice Muffins

1 Preheat oven to 400°F. Grease 12 standard (2 1/2-inch) muffin cups. Combine flours, baking powder, baking soda, salt and cinnamon in medium bowl; mix well.

2 Attach flat beater to stand mixer. Place brown sugar and butter in mixer bowl; beat on high until creamy. Beat in egg until well blended. Add 1/2 cup milk; beat in well. Mix in wild rice on low. Add flour mixture in two additions, beating on medium just until blended. Batter should be somewhat wet; if too stiff, add remaining milk, 1 tablespoon at a time. Stir in pecans and dates.

3 Spoon batter into prepared muffin cups, filling three-fourths full. Bake 12 to 15 minutes or until toothpick inserted into centers comes out clean. Cool in pan 2 minutes; remove to wire rack.

1/2 cup all-purpose flour
1/2 cup whole wheat flour
1 1/2 teaspoons baking powder
1 teaspoon baking soda
1/4 teaspoon salt
1/4 teaspoon ground cinnamon
1/3 cup packed dark brown sugar
1/4 cup (1/2 stick) unsalted butter, softened
1 egg
1/2 to 2/3 cup milk
1 cup cooked wild rice
1/2 cup coarsely chopped pecans
1/2 cup pitted chopped dates

117

Rosemary Lager Focaccia

MAKES 12 SERVINGS

1¼ cups lager or nonalcoholic beer

4 tablespoons extra virgin olive oil, divided

1 package (¼ ounce) active dry yeast

1 tablespoon sugar

3 cups plus ¼ cup all-purpose flour, divided

2 teaspoons coarse salt, divided

¼ cup fresh rosemary leaves

1 Place lager in medium microwavable bowl. Microwave on HIGH 25 seconds. Stir in 3 tablespoons oil, yeast and sugar; let stand 5 minutes or until foamy.

2 Attach dough hook to stand mixer. Place 3 cups flour and 1 teaspoon salt in mixer bowl. Stir in lager mixture on low until dough pulls away from sides of bowl. Knead on low until smooth, elastic and slightly sticky, adding remaining flour 1 tablespoon at a time if needed. Shape dough into a ball. Place in large lightly greased bowl; turn once to grease surface. Cover; let rise in warm place 1½ hours or until doubled.

3 Grease baking sheet. Place dough on prepared baking sheet; stretch into 15×10-inch rectangle. Cover; let stand 30 minutes. Preheat oven to 325°F.

4 Brush dough with remaining 1 tablespoon oil. Sprinkle with rosemary and remaining 1 teaspoon salt. Bake 30 minutes or until golden brown. Cool 10 minutes before slicing. Serve warm or at room temperature.

Note: To reheat, wrap leftovers in foil and warm 10 minutes in a 300°F oven.

Vegetable Bliss

Discover delicious new ways to eat your vegetables. Why settle for ordinary french fries? With a little help from your KitchenAid® stand mixer and the Rotor Slicer/Shredder you can make Exotic Veggie Chips instead. And you certainly don't need to be a vegetarian to appreciate an elegant Spinach Soufflé or homemade Hummus.

When it comes to color, texture and variety, vegetables have meat beat! Add some new flavor to your life with kohlrabi, plantains or tomatillos. The recipes in this chapter will show you how. With the Food Grinder you can easily create fresh salsa or falafel that will top most restaurant versions. The Fruit/Vegetable strainer lets you turn a simple can of chickpeas into delicious hummus in a matter of minutes.

Make your veggies more than just a side dish.

Exotic Veggie Chips

3 tropical tubers (malanga, yautia, lila and/or taro roots)*

1 or 2 yellow (unripe) plantains

2 parsnips, peeled

1 medium sweet potato, peeled

1 lotus root,** peeled

Oil for deep frying

Coarse salt

These tropical tubers are all similar and their labels are frequently interchangeable or overlapping. They are available in the produce sections of Latin markets. Choose whichever tubers are available and fresh. Look for firm roots without signs of mildew or soft spots.

**Lotus root is available in produce sections of Asian markets. The outside looks like a fat beige link sausage, but when sliced, the lacy, snowflake-like pattern inside is revealed.*

1 Line two baking sheets with paper towels. Peel thick shaggy skin from tubers, rinse and dry. Cut tubers into 3-inch lengths.

2 Assemble Rotor Slicer/Shredder with thin slicing cone; attach to stand mixer. Slice tubers and place in single layer on prepared baking sheets to absorb excess moisture. (Stack in multiple layers with paper towels between layers.) Peel thick skin from plantain. Slice and arrange on paper towels. Slice parsnips and sweet potato and transfer to paper towels. Trim lotus root and remove tough skin with paring knife; slice and transfer to paper towels.

3 Fill deep fryer or deep, heavy pot with oil and heat over medium-high heat to 350°F. Working in batches, deep fry each vegetable until crisp and slightly curled, stirring occasionally. Frying time will vary from 2 to 6 minutes depending on the vegetable. Remove vegetables with slotted spoon and drain on paper towels; immediately sprinkle with salt.

4 Once drained and cooled, combine chips. Serve at once or store in airtight containers at room temperature. To recrisp chips, bake in preheated 350°F oven 5 minutes.

124

Black Bean Flautas with Charred Tomatillo Salsa

SALSA

1 **pound tomatillos, husked and quartered**

1 **small yellow onion, peeled, cut into wedges**

6 **cloves garlic, unpeeled**

1 **jalapeño pepper, halved**

Juice of $^1/_2$ **lime**

Salt and black pepper

FLAUTAS

10 **ounces Colby Jack cheese, partially frozen**

1 **can (about 15 ounces) black beans, undrained**

1 **teaspoon salt, divided**

$^1/_2$ **teaspoon ground cumin**

$^1/_2$ **teaspoon chili powder**

3 **cloves garlic, minced**

$^1/_4$ **cup chopped fresh cilantro**

Juice of 1 lime

10 **(6-inch) flour tortillas**

1 **cup seeded and chopped tomatoes**

1 **cup thinly sliced green onions**

SALSA

1 For salsa, char tomatillos, onion, garlic and jalapeño in dry heavy skillet over medium-high heat about 5 minutes or until soft and blackened in patches. Remove from skillet; cool 5 minutes. Peel garlic; remove stem and seeds from jalapeño. Assemble Food Grinder with coarse grinding plate; attach to stand mixer. Grind tomatillos, onion, jalapeños and garlic into bowl. Stir in lime juice and season with salt and pepper. Refrigerate until ready to serve.

FLAUTAS

2 Remove grinder; assemble Rotor Slicer/Shredder with coarse shredding cone and attach to mixer. Shred cheese into bowl.

3 Place beans and liquid, $^1/_2$ teaspoon salt, cumin, chili powder and garlic in medium saucepan. Bring to a boil over medium-high heat. Reduce heat; simmer 10 minutes or until beans are very soft. Purée bean mixture, cilantro, lime juice and remaining $^1/_2$ teaspoon salt in food processor or blender.

4 Preheat oven to 450°F. Spread bean purée evenly on each tortilla; sprinkle with cheese, tomatoes and green onions. Roll up tightly and place seam side down in 13×9-inch baking dish.

5 Bake 10 to 15 minutes or until crisp and brown and cheese is melted. Serve with salsa.

Spinach Soufflé

1 pound fresh spinach leaves

¹/₄ cup (¹/₂ stick) butter

1 tablespoon finely chopped shallot

¹/₄ cup all-purpose flour

¹/₄ teaspoon salt

¹/₄ teaspoon ground nutmeg

¹/₈ teaspoon ground white pepper

1¹/₂ cups milk, at room temperature

6 eggs, separated

¹/₂ cup freshly grated Parmesan cheese

Pinch cream of tartar (optional)

1 Preheat oven to 375°F. Grease 2-quart soufflé dish or deep casserole.

2 Bring large pot of salted water to a boil over high heat. Add spinach; cook 1 to 2 minutes or until wilted. Drain and immediately plunge into cold water to stop cooking. When cool enough to handle, squeeze out excess moisture. Finely chop spinach.

3 Melt butter in large saucepan over medium heat. Add shallot; sauté 2 to 3 minutes. Whisk in flour, salt, nutmeg and pepper. Gradually whisk in milk. Whisk until mixture boils and thickens. Let cool slightly.

4 Stir egg yolks into saucepan until well blended. Add spinach and cheese; mix well.

5 Attach wire whip to stand mixer. Place egg whites in mixer bowl with cream of tartar. Beat on high until egg whites form stiff peaks.

6 Gently fold egg whites into spinach mixture until almost combined. (Some white streaks should remain.) Transfer mixture to prepared dish.

7 Bake 30 to 40 minutes or until puffed and golden and wooden skewer inserted into center comes out moist but clean. Serve immediately.

128

Hummus

1 Assemble Food Grinder with Fruit/Vegetable Strainer and attach to stand mixer. Strain chickpeas into mixer bowl; collect pulp in another bowl. Add pulp, water, lemon juice, tahini, garlic, salt and paprika to mixer bowl.

2 Remove strainer and attach wire whip. Whip on medium 1 minute. Stop and scrape bowl. Whip on high 1 minute or until smooth. Transfer hummus to serving bowl.

3 Combine tomato, onions and parsley; spoon over hummus.

- **1 can (20 ounces) chickpeas, drained**
- **¼ cup cold water**
- **¼ cup fresh lemon juice**
- **¼ cup tahini**
- **3 cloves garlic, minced**
- **½ teaspoon salt**
- **¼ teaspoon paprika (optional)**
- **1 tomato, finely chopped**
- **2 green onions, finely chopped**
- **2 tablespoons chopped fresh parsley**

129

Spaghetti with Cauliflower & Feta

● **MAKES 4 SERVINGS**

1 **recipe Whole Wheat Dough
for Pasta Press cut into
spaghetti or bucatini
(page 85)** *or* **1 package
(about 13 ounces) dried
whole wheat spaghetti**

3 **tablespoons olive oil**

1 **onion chopped**

4 **cloves garlic, minced**

1 **head cauliflower, cut into
bite-size florets**

²/₃ **cup white wine or water**

1 **teaspoon salt**

¹/₂ **teaspoon black pepper**

1 **pint grape tomatoes, cut in
half**

¹/₂ **cup coarsely chopped
walnuts**

¹/₄ **teaspoon red pepper flakes**

¹/₂ **cup crumbled feta cheese**

1 Prepare pasta with pasta press.

2 Heat oil in large skillet over medium heat. Add onion; sauté 3 minutes or until soft. Add garlic; sauté 2 minutes. Add cauliflower; sauté 5 minutes. Add wine, salt and pepper. Cover and cook about 10 minutes or until cauliflower is crisp-tender.

3 Add tomatoes, walnuts and red pepper flakes to skillet. Cook 2 to 3 minutes or until tomatoes begin to soften.

4 Meanwhile, bring large pot of salted water to a boil. Cook fresh pasta 1 to 2 minutes or dried pasta according to package directions until barely tender. Drain; reserve ¹/₂ cup pasta cooking water and stir into sauce. Toss spaghetti with sauce in skillet or serving bowl. Top with feta.

**menu
ideas**

FRESH FROM THE FARMERS' MARKET

●

Spaghetti with Cauliflower & Feta

Potato-Zucchini Pancakes with Warm Corn Salsa, 136

Fresh Raspberry Sorbet, 153

130

Tofu Rigatoni Casserole

1 recipe Eggless Dough
  for Pasta Press cut into
  rigatoni (page 83) *or*
  16 ounces dried rigatoni

4 ounces Asiago cheese,
  partially frozen

4 ounces mozzarella cheese,
  partially frozen

4 cups loosely packed baby
  spinach

1 cup soft tofu

1 egg

$^1/_4$ teaspoon salt

$^1/_4$ teaspoon black pepper

$^1/_4$ teaspoon ground nutmeg

1 can (about 14 ounces) diced
  tomatoes with basil, garlic
  and oregano*

1 can (about 14 ounces)
  quartered artichokes,
  drained and chopped

*Or substitute 1 can (about 14 ounces)
unseasoned diced tomatoes and add
$^1/_2$ teaspoon each dried garlic, basil
and oregano.*

1 Prepare pasta with Pasta Press. Assemble Rotor Slicer/Shredder with coarse shredding cone; attach to stand mixer. Shred cheeses into bowl. Grease 11×7-inch baking dish.

2 Bring large pot of salted water to a boil. Cook fresh rigatoni 2 to 3 minutes or dried rigatoni according to package directions until barely tender. Drain; return to saucepan. Stir in spinach.

3 Combine tofu, egg, salt, pepper and nutmeg in medium bowl; mix until blended. Fold tofu mixture into rigatoni. Add tomatoes, artichokes and 1$^1/_2$ cups cheese; mix well. Spoon into prepared baking dish.

4 Bake 20 minutes. Top with remaining cheese. Bake 10 minutes or until cheese is melted.

134

Kohlrabi & Carrot Slaw

1 Assemble Rotor Slicer/Shredder with coarse shredding cone; attach to stand mixer. Shred kohlrabi and carrots into mixer bowl. Add bell pepper, tomatoes and green onions.

2 Combine mayonnaise, yogurt, vinegar, parsley, dill, salt, cumin and black pepper in small bowl until smooth. Add to vegetables; toss to coat. Cover; refrigerate until ready to serve.

- **2 pounds kohlrabi bulbs, peeled**
- **4 medium carrots**
- **1 red bell pepper, chopped**
- **1 pint grape tomatoes, halved**
- **2 green onions, thinly sliced**
- **$1/3$ cup mayonnaise**
- **$1/3$ cup plain yogurt**
- **2 tablespoons cider vinegar**
- **2 tablespoons finely chopped fresh parsley**
- **1 teaspoon dried dill weed**
- **$1/4$ teaspoon salt**
- **$1/4$ teaspoon ground cumin**
- **$1/8$ teaspoon black pepper**

• **135**

Potato-Zucchini Pancakes with Warm Corn Salsa

Warm Corn Salsa
(recipe follows)
3 **russet potatoes, peeled**
2 **large zucchini**
2 **eggs**
1/4 **cup all-purpose flour**
2 **tablespoons chopped onion**
2 **tablespoons chopped green bell pepper**
1/2 **teaspoon salt**
1/4 **teaspoon black pepper**
Vegetable oil

136

1 Prepare Warm Corn Salsa; keep warm.

2 Assemble Rotor Slicer/Shredder with coarse shredding cone; attach to stand mixer. Shred potatoes and zucchini into mixer bowl. Squeeze all moisture from vegetables in colander. Return to bowl. Add eggs, flour, onion, bell pepper, salt and black pepper; stir until blended.

3 Heat 1/4 inch of oil in large skillet over medium high heat. Pat handfuls of mixture into cakes about 3 inches in diameter. Cook in batches without crowding pan 3 minutes per side until firm and browned. Serve with Warm Corn Salsa.

Warm Corn Salsa

1 **tablespoon olive oil**
2 **tablespoons chopped onion**
2 **tablespoons finely chopped green bell pepper**
1 **package (9 ounces) frozen corn, thawed**
1 **cup chunky salsa**
2 **teaspoons chopped fresh cilantro**

Heat oil in medium skillet. Add onion and bell pepper; sauté 3 minutes or until crisp-tender. Add corn, salsa and cilantro. Reduce heat to medium-low. Cook 5 minutes or until hot.

• **MAKES 3 CUPS**

Falafel with Garlic Tahini Sauce

MAKES 8 SERVINGS

1 cup dried chickpeas, sorted and rinsed

Garlic Tahini Sauce (recipe follows)

1 small onion, cut into wedges

2 cloves garlic

1/2 cup chopped fresh parsley

2 teaspoons ground cumin

1 teaspoon ground coriander

1/2 teaspoon salt

1/2 teaspoon ground red pepper

1 tablespoon lemon juice

Vegetable oil

Pita Bread (page 120), tomatoes and chopped cucumbers

1 Soak chickpeas overnight in large bowl with water to cover by at least 3 inches. (Chickpeas will triple in volume.) Prepare Garlic Tahini Sauce; refrigerate until ready to serve.

2 Drain chickpeas. Assemble Food Grinder with fine grinding plate; attach to stand mixer. Grind chickpeas, onion and garlic into mixer bowl. Add parsley, cumin, coriander, salt, red pepper and lemon juice. Remove Food Grinder and attach flat beater; beat until smooth. If mixture is too dry, add 1 to 2 tablespoons water.

3 Shape heaping tablespoons of mixture into 1 1/2-inch balls with dampened hands. Place on baking sheet lined with waxed paper. Refrigerate until ready to cook.

4 Pour oil into deep heavy saucepan to depth of 2 inches. Heat over medium-high heat to 350°F. Fry falafel in batches 3 to 5 minutes or until golden brown. Remove with slotted spoon and drain on paper towels.

5 Serve with Garlic Tahini Sauce, pita bread, lettuce, tomatoes and cucumbers.

Garlic Tahini Sauce: Attach wire whip to stand mixer. Combine 1/2 cup plain whole milk yogurt, 1/2 cup tahini, 3 tablespoons water, 2 tablespoons fresh lemon juice, 1 minced garlic clove and 1/2 teaspoon ground cumin in mixer bowl. Season with salt and pepper. Whip until blended. Cover; refrigerate 1 hour. Makes about 1 cup.

138

Sweet Treats

Your sweet tooth has come to the right place. With your KitchenAid®
stand mixer, dessert is a piece of cake—or pie, or maybe a bowl of ice
cream, or cookies! For traditionalists there are recipes for Apple Cake
and Tart Cherry Pie, while more adventurous palates will appreciate
Espresso Gelato and the addictive Mexican pastries called Sopaipillas.

Fancy frozen treats are a cinch when you have the Ice Cream Maker
tucked away in your freezer. Fruit lovers will adore Creamy Lemon-
Orange Gelato and Fresh Raspberry Sorbet. And never underestimate
how the aroma of freshly baked cookies or gingerbread cooling on the
counter can draw a happy, hungry crowd. The recipes in this chapter will
give everyone plenty of great reasons to eat dessert first.

Rocky Road Ice Cream

- **MAKES ABOUT 1³/₄ QUARTS**

²/₃ **cup unsweetened Dutch process cocoa powder**

¹/₄ **cup boiling water**

1¹/₂ **cups whole milk**

1¹/₂ **cups heavy whipping cream**

6 **egg yolks**

1 **cup sugar**

2 **ounces unsweetened chocolate, finely chopped**

1 **teaspoon vanilla**

1¹/₂ **cups miniature marshmallows**

³/₄ **cup toasted and coarsely chopped walnuts***

*To toast walnuts, spread in single layer on baking sheet. Bake in preheated 350°F oven 8 to 10 minutes or until golden brown, stirring frequently.

142

ICE CREAM SOCIAL

•

Rocky Road Ice Cream

Fresh Strawberry Ice Cream, 144

Candy Bar Ice Cream, 146

Butter Almond Ice Cream with Amaretto Caramel Sauce, 172

1 Place cocoa powder in heavy medium saucepan; whisk in boiling water to make paste. Whisk in milk and cream. Bring to a simmer over medium heat, whisking often. Remove from heat.

2 Attach flat beater to stand mixer. Beat yolks and sugar in mixer bowl on low 1 minute or until pale and thickened. Gradually beat in milk mixture. Return entire mixture to saucepan and cook over medium-low heat, stirring constantly with wooden spoon, until custard lightly coats spoon and instant-read thermometer reads 185°F.

3 Place chopped chocolate in large bowl and place wire sieve over bowl. Immediately strain custard through sieve over chocolate. Let stand 3 minutes, then whisk until chocolate is melted and smooth. Stir in vanilla. Cover and refrigerate 2 hours or until well chilled.

4 Attach frozen Ice Cream Maker bowl and dasher to stand mixer. Turn mixer to stir; pour cold mixture into bowl with mixer running. Continue to stir 20 to 30 minutes or until consistency of soft-serve ice cream. Remove dasher and stir in marshmallows and nuts with wooden spoon.

5 Transfer ice cream to airtight container; freeze several hours until firm.

Fresh Strawberry Ice Cream

MAKES 2 QUARTS

2 1/2 cups half-and-half

8 egg yolks

1 cup plus 2 teaspoons sugar, divided

2 1/2 cups heavy whipping cream

4 teaspoons vanilla

1/8 teaspoon salt

2 cups chopped fresh strawberries (or other fresh fruit)

1 Heat half-and-half in medium saucepan over medium heat until bubbles form around edge of pan, stirring often. Do not boil. Remove from heat.

2 Attach flat beater to stand mixer. Place egg yolks and 1 cup sugar in mixer bowl; beat on low about 1 minute or until well blended and slightly thickened. Very gradually add warm half-and-half at low speed; mix until blended. Return mixture to same saucepan; cook over medium heat until small bubbles form around edge and mixture is steamy, stirring constantly. Do not boil. Transfer mixture to large bowl; stir in cream, vanilla and salt. Cover and refrigerate 2 hours or until well chilled.

3 Combine strawberries and remaining 2 teaspoons sugar in medium bowl. Attach frozen Ice Cream Maker bowl and dasher to stand mixer. Turn mixer to stir; pour cold mixture into bowl with mixer running. Continue to stir 20 to 30 minutes or until consistency of soft-serve ice cream. Add strawberries during last 3 to 5 minutes of mixing.

4 Transfer ice cream to airtight container and freeze several hours or until firm.

French Vanilla Ice Cream: Omit strawberries and extra 2 teaspoons sugar.

Cookies & Cream Ice Cream: Prepare French Vanilla Ice Cream. Add 1 1/2 cups chopped cream-filled chocolate sandwich cookies (or other cookies, nuts or candies) during last 1 to 2 minutes of mixing.

Candy Bar Ice Cream

2½ cups half-and-half

¾ cup sugar

1 cup heavy whipping cream

2 teaspoons vanilla

1½ cups chopped (½ inch or smaller pieces) candy bars, such as chocolate-covered toffee or peanut butter cups

1 Heat 1 cup half-and-half and sugar in medium saucepan over medium heat until bubbles form around edge of pan, stirring often to dissolve sugar. Pour into heatproof medium bowl set in larger bowl of iced water. Stir in remaining 1½ cups half-and-half, cream and vanilla.

2 Let stand 1 hour or until chilled, stirring often and adding more ice as needed. Or cover and refrigerate overnight.

3 Attach frozen Ice Cream Maker bowl and dasher to stand mixer. Turn mixer to stir; pour cold mixture into bowl with mixer running. Continue to stir 20 to 30 minutes or until consistency of soft-serve ice cream. Stir in candy during last 2 minutes of mixing.

4 Transfer ice cream to airtight container and freeze several hours until firm. This ice cream is best served within 24 hours of churning.

146

Apple Cake

1 Preheat oven to 350°F. Grease 13×9-inch baking pan.

2 Attach flat beater to stand mixer. Place ³/₄ cup granulated sugar, butter, brown sugar, eggs and vanilla in mixer bowl; beat on medium 3 minutes or until creamy. Beat in buttermilk.

3 Combine flour, 1 teaspoon cinnamon, baking powder, baking soda, salt and nutmeg in medium bowl. Beat into sugar mixture until well blended. Stir in apples.

4 Pour batter into prepared pan. Combine remaining ¹/₂ cup granulated sugar, remaining 1 teaspoon cinnamon and nuts in small bowl. Sprinkle over batter.

5 Bake 35 to 40 minutes or until toothpick inserted in center comes out clean. Cool completely on wire rack.

1¼ **cups granulated sugar, divided**

1 **cup (2 sticks) butter, softened**

³/₄ **cup packed brown sugar**

2 **eggs**

1 **teaspoon vanilla**

1 **cup buttermilk**

2¹/₂ **cups all-purpose flour**

2 **teaspoons ground cinnamon, divided**

1 **teaspoon baking powder**

1 **teaspoon baking soda**

1 **teaspoon salt**

¹/₄ **teaspoon ground nutmeg**

3 **cups chopped peeled apples**

1 **cup chopped nuts**

147

Gingerbread with Lemon Sauce

MAKES 9 SERVINGS

2½ cups all-purpose flour

1½ teaspoons ground cinnamon

1 teaspoon ground ginger

½ teaspoon baking soda

½ teaspoon salt

½ cup (1 stick) butter, softened

¾ cup packed light brown sugar

⅓ cup light molasses

1 egg

¾ cup stout or other dark beer, at room temperature

Lemon Sauce (recipe follows)

Grated lemon peel (optional)

148

1 Preheat oven to 350°F. Grease 9-inch square baking pan. Combine flour, cinnamon, ginger, baking soda and salt in medium bowl.

2 Attach flat beater to stand mixer. Place butter and brown sugar in mixer bowl; beat on medium until light and fluffy. Add molasses and egg; beat well. Add flour mixture alternately with stout, beating after each addition. Pour batter evenly into prepared pan.

3 Bake 35 to 40 minutes or until toothpick inserted in center comes out clean. Cool on wire rack.

4 Prepare Lemon Sauce. Top gingerbread with Lemon Sauce and sprinkle with grated lemon peel.

Lemon Sauce

1 cup granulated sugar

½ cup (1 stick) butter

¾ cup heavy whipping cream

1 tablespoon lemon juice

2 teaspoons grated lemon peel

1 Combine granulated sugar, butter and cream in small saucepan. Cook over medium heat until butter is melted, stirring constantly.

2 Reduce heat to low; simmer 5 minutes. Stir in lemon juice and lemon peel. Cool slightly.

menu ideas

HOLIDAY ENTERTAINING

Espresso Gelato

2½ cups whole milk

1 cup heavy whipping cream

¾ cup very coarsely ground espresso or dark roast coffee beans

1 cup sugar

3 egg yolks

1 tablespoon plus 2 teaspoons cornstarch

1 teaspoon vanilla

1 cup mini chocolate chips (optional)

1 Heat milk, cream and espresso beans in heavy medium saucepan over medium heat until bubbles form around edge of pan. Do not boil. Remove from heat and let steep 10 minutes.

2 Whisk sugar, egg yolks and cornstarch in large bowl. Gradually whisk in hot espresso mixture. Rinse saucepan. Pour cream mixture into saucepan. Cook over medium heat, whisking constantly until mixture is barely simmering (cornstarch will prevent curdling). Strain through fine mesh sieve into medium bowl. Stir in vanilla. Refrigerate 2 hours or until well chilled.

3 Attach frozen Ice Cream Maker bowl and dasher to stand mixer. Turn mixer to stir; pour cold mixture into bowl with mixer running. Continue to stir 20 to 30 minutes or until consistency of soft serve ice cream. Mix in chocolate chips during last 2 minutes, if desired.

4 Transfer gelato to airtight container and freeze 2 hours or until firm.

150

Chocolate Chip Banana Bread

1 Preheat oven to 350°F. Grease four mini (5^1/$_2$×3-inch) or three medium (7^1/$_2$×3^1/$_2$-inch) loaf pans.

2 Attach flat beater to stand mixer. Place flour, granulated sugar, brown sugar, baking powder and salt in mixer bowl; mix well. Beat in bananas, milk, peanut butter, oil, egg and vanilla until well blended. Stir in chocolate chips just until moistened. Pour into prepared pans.

3 Bake 40 minutes or until toothpick inserted into centers comes out clean (45 to 50 minutes for medium pans). Cool in pans 10 minutes. Remove from pans; cool completely on wire racks.

2^1/$_2$ **cups all-purpose flour**
^{1}/$_2$ **cup granulated sugar**
^{1}/$_2$ **cup packed brown sugar**
1 **tablespoon baking powder**
^{3}/$_4$ **teaspoon salt**
1 **cup mashed ripe bananas (about 2 large)**
1 **cup milk**
^{3}/$_4$ **cup peanut butter**
^{1}/$_4$ **cup vegetable oil**
1 **egg, lightly beaten**
1 **teaspoon vanilla**
1 **cup semisweet chocolate chips**

151

Sopaipillas

- **MAKES 16 SOPAIPILLAS**

$^1/_4$ **cup plus 2 teaspoons sugar, divided**

$^1/_2$ **teaspoon ground cinnamon**

  2 cups all-purpose flour

  2 teaspoons baking powder

$^1/_2$ **teaspoon salt**

  2 tablespoons shortening

$^3/_4$ **cup warm water**

  Vegetable oil for deep-frying

  Honey

1 Combine $^1/_4$ cup sugar and cinnamon in small bowl; set aside. Attach flat beater to stand mixer. Place remaining 2 teaspoons sugar, flour, baking powder and salt in mixer bowl. Cut in shortening on low until mixture resembles fine crumbs. Gradually add water; stir until mixture forms dough. Replace beater with dough hook; knead 2 minutes on low until smooth. Shape into a ball on lightly floured surface. Cover with bowl and let rest 30 minutes.

2 Divide dough into four pieces; shape each piece into a ball. Roll each ball into 8-inch circle $^1/_8$ inch thick. Cut each round into four wedges.

3 Pour oil into deep heavy saucepan or electric skillet to depth of $1^1/_2$ inches. Heat to 360°F. Cook dough in batches 1 minute per side or until puffed and golden brown. Drain on paper towels. Sprinkle with cinnamon-sugar mixture. Serve hot drizzled with honey.

Fresh Raspberry Sorbet

1 Prepare Simple Syrup. Assemble Food Grinder with Fruit / Vegetable Strainer. Place raspberries in hopper and strain into mixer bowl. Collect pulp in another bowl. Return pulp to hopper and strain again into mixer bowl. Discard remaining pulp.

2 Stir in Simple Syrup. Refrigerate 2 hours or until thoroughly chilled.

3 Attach frozen Ice Cream Maker bowl and dasher to stand mixer. Turn mixer to stir; pour cold mixture into bowl with mixer running. Continue to stir 12 to 15 minutes or until consistency of soft serve ice cream.

4 Transfer sorbet to airtight container and freeze several hours.

Simple Syrup: Combine 1¹⁄₂ cups water and 1¹⁄₄ cups sugar in saucepan. Bring to a boil over medium-high heat; cook and stir 10 minutes or until sugar dissolves completely. Transfer to ice bath, stirring until well chilled. Refrigerate until ready to use.

6 **cups raspberries**
1¹⁄₄ **cups Simple Syrup (recipe follows)**

● 153

Mocha-Cinnamon Blondies

MAKES 36 SERVINGS

1	cup (2 sticks) unsalted butter, softened
1³/₄	cups sugar
4	eggs
1	cup all-purpose flour
2	teaspoons instant coffee granules
1	teaspoon ground cinnamon
¹/₄	teaspoon salt
1	cup chopped pecans
³/₄	cup semisweet chocolate chips

1 Preheat oven to 350°F. Grease 13×9-inch baking pan.

2 Attach flat beater to stand mixer. Place butter, sugar and eggs in mixer bowl; beat on medium until light and fluffy. Add flour, coffee, cinnamon and salt; beat on low until combined. Stir in pecans and chocolate chips. Spread batter in prepared pan.

3 Bake 30 minutes or until sides begin to pull away from pan. Cool completely in pan on wire rack.

Creamy Lemon-Orange Gelato

1 Heat milk, orange peel, lemon peel and coffee beans in heavy medium saucepan over medium heat until bubbles form around edge of pan. Do not boil. Remove from heat.

2 Whisk yolks and sugar in medium bowl. Gradually whisk half of milk mixture into yolks. Return mixture to saucepan with remaining milk. Stir over low heat about 8 minutes or until mixture thickens slightly and leaves path on back of spoon when finger is drawn across; do not boil. Strain through fine mesh sieve into bowl. Refrigerate 2 hours or until well chilled.

3 Attach frozen Ice Cream Maker bowl and dasher to stand mixer. Turn mixer to stir; pour cold mixture into bowl with mixer running. Continue to stir 15 to 20 minutes or until consistency of soft serve ice cream.

4 Transfer ice cream to airtight container and freeze several hours or until frozen.

2 **cups milk**
4 **(2×³/₄-inch) strips orange peel**
4 **(2×³/₄-inch) strips lemon peel**
6 **coffee beans**
5 **egg yolks**
³/₄ **cup sugar**

155

Pear Spice Cake

4 cups chopped peeled pears
2 cups granulated sugar
1 cup chopped walnuts
3 cups all-purpose flour
2 teaspoons baking soda
³/₄ teaspoon ground cinnamon
¹/₂ teaspoon salt
¹/₄ teaspoon ground nutmeg
¹/₈ teaspoon ground cloves
2 eggs
1 cup vegetable oil
1¹/₂ teaspoons vanilla
  Powdered sugar

1 Combine pears, granulated sugar and walnuts in medium bowl; mix lightly. Let stand 1 hour, stirring occasionally.

2 Preheat oven to 375°F. Grease and flour 10-inch fluted tube pan.

3 Attach flat beater to stand mixer. Combine flour, baking soda, cinnamon, salt, nutmeg and cloves in mixer bowl. Beat in eggs, oil and vanilla. Add pear mixture; mix well. Pour into prepared pan.

4 Bake 1 hour and 15 minutes or until toothpick inserted near center comes out clean. Cool in pan 10 minutes. Loosen edges and remove to rack to cool completely.

5 Dust lightly with powdered sugar before serving.

156

Extra-Chocolatey Brownie Cookies

1 Preheat oven to 375°F. Whisk flour, cocoa, baking soda and salt in medium bowl until well blended.

2 Attach flat beater to stand mixer. Place butter and sugars in mixer bowl; beat on medium until light and fluffy. Beat in eggs, and vanilla until well blended. Add flour mixture; beat on low until blended. Stir in chocolate chunks and walnuts. Drop dough by heaping tablespoonfuls 2 inches apart onto ungreased cookie sheets; flatten slightly.

3 Bake 12 minutes or until set. Cool on cookie sheets 2 minutes. Remove to wire racks; cool completely.

2 **cups all-purpose flour**
¹/₂ **cup unsweetened Dutch process cocoa powder**
1 **teaspoon baking soda**
³/₄ **teaspoon salt**
1 **cup (2 sticks) butter, softened**
1 **cup packed brown sugar**
¹/₂ **cup granulated sugar**
2 **eggs**
2 **teaspoons vanilla**
1 **package (11¹/₂ ounces) semisweet chocolate chunks**
2 **cups coarsely chopped walnuts or pecans**

menu ideas

GAME DAY

Chipotle Beer Fondue, 47

Pork & Parmesan Sausages, 74

Mac & Cheesiest, 95

Bacon-Jalapeño Corn Bread, 116

Extra-Chocolatey Brownie Cookies

Plum Cobbler with Cinnamon Drop Biscuits

6 cups sliced unpeeled ripe plums (about 12 medium)

1 cup plus 2 tablespoons all-purpose flour, divided

8 tablespoons granulated sugar, divided

1/4 cup packed brown sugar

1 tablespoon lemon juice

2 teaspoons baking powder

1/2 teaspoon ground cinnamon

1/4 teaspoon salt

1/4 cup (1/2 stick) cold unsalted butter, cubed

1/2 cup plus 2 tablespoons milk

1 Preheat oven to 400°F. Butter 8-inch square baking dish.

2 Combine plums, 2 tablespoons flour, 6 tablespoons granulated sugar, brown sugar and lemon juice in large bowl. Toss until well blended. Transfer to prepared baking dish. Bake 10 minutes.

3 Attach flat beater to stand mixer. Place remaining 1 cup flour, 2 tablespoons granulated sugar, baking powder, cinnamon and salt in mixer bowl. Cut in butter on low until mixture resembles coarse crumbs. Gradually add 1/2 cup milk, stirring until sticky dough forms. Add additional 2 tablespoons milk if needed.

4 Drop heaping tablespoonfuls of dough over plum mixture. Bake 20 minutes or until golden brown. Serve warm.

Lots o' Chocolate Bread

1 Preheat oven to 350°F. Grease 5 mini (5¹/₂×3-inch) loaf pans. Place 1 cup chocolate chips in small microwavable bowl. Microwave on HIGH 1 minute; stir. Microwave at 30-second intervals, stirring after each interval, until chocolate is melted.

2 Attach flat beater to stand mixer. Place brown sugar and butter in mixer bowl; beat on medium until creamy. Add melted chocolate and eggs; beat until well blended. Add flour, applesauce, vanilla, baking soda, baking powder and salt; beat until well blended. Stir in ¹/₂ cup chocolate chips. Spoon batter evenly into prepared pans.

3 Bake 35 to 40 minutes or until centers crack and are dry to the touch. Cool in pans on wire racks 10 minutes. Remove from pans; cool completely.

4 Place remaining ¹/₂ cup chocolate chips and shortening in small microwavable bowl. Microwave on HIGH 1 minute; stir. Microwave at 30-second intervals, stirring after each interval, until chocolate is melted and mixture is smooth. Drizzle loaves with glaze; let stand until set.

Gift Idea: Wrap each loaf in plastic wrap or cellophane and place in a colorful gift bag. With each loaf include packets of gourmet coffee or tea.

- **2 cups mini semisweet chocolate chips, divided**
- **²/₃ cup packed light brown sugar**
- **¹/₂ cup (1 stick) butter, softened**
- **2 eggs**
- **2¹/₂ cups all-purpose flour**
- **1¹/₂ cups applesauce**
- **1¹/₂ teaspoons vanilla**
- **1 teaspoon baking soda**
- **1 teaspoon baking powder**
- **¹/₂ teaspoon salt**
- **1 tablespoon shortening (do not use butter, margarine, spread or oil)**

159

Butterscotch Oatmeal Cookies

• **MAKES ABOUT 3 DOZEN COOKIES**

1¼ cups all-purpose flour
½ teaspoon salt
½ teaspoon baking soda
½ cup butterscotch chips
½ cup (1 stick) butter,
    softened
½ cup packed brown sugar
¼ cup granulated sugar
1 egg, lightly beaten
1 teaspoon vanilla
¾ cup old-fashioned oats
½ cup shredded coconut
½ cup chopped pecans
    Pecan halves (about 36)

1 Preheat oven to 350°F. Lightly grease cookie sheets. Combine flour, salt and baking soda in medium bowl.

2 Place butterscotch chips in small microwavable bowl. Microwave on HIGH 1 minute; stir. Microwave at additional 30-second intervals until chips are melted and smooth.

3 Attach flat beater to stand mixer. Place butter, brown sugar and granulated sugar in mixer bowl; beat on medium until light and fluffy. Beat in egg, melted butterscotch chips and vanilla until well blended. Add flour mixture; beat just until blended. Stir in oats, coconut and chopped pecans.

4 Shape level tablespoonfuls of dough into balls; place 2 inches apart on prepared cookie sheets. Press 1 pecan half into center of each ball.

5 Bake 10 minutes or until edges are lightly browned. Cool on cookie sheets 1 minute. Remove to wire racks; cool completely.

160

Tart Cherry Pie

1 Prepare pastry.

2 Preheat oven to 425°F. Drain cherries, reserving ¹/₂ cup juice. Place cherries and reserved juice in large bowl. Combine granulated sugar, tapioca, cinnamon and lemon peel in small bowl. Add to cherries; mix well. Set aside.

3 Roll out one portion of pastry into 12-inch circle on floured surface. Line 9-inch pie pan with pastry.

4 Roll out remaining pastry into 11-inch circle on floured surface. Make slits in pastry with sharp knife.

5 Pour cherry mixture into crust; sprinkle evenly with butter cubes. Top with second crust; fold edge under and seal. Flute edge.

6 Brush top crust lightly with egg mixture; sprinkle with coarse sugar. Place pie on baking sheet.

7 Bake 15 minutes. Reduce oven temperature to 350°F. Bake 30 to 35 minutes or until crust is golden and juices are bubbly, covering loosely with foil during last 10 minutes of baking to prevent overbrowning. Cool on wire rack. Serve warm or at room temperature.

Pie Pastry for Two-Crust Pie (page 182)

2 **cans (about 14 ounces each) tart cherries, packed in water**

1¹/₂ **cups granulated sugar**

¹/₄ **cup quick-cooking tapioca**

1 **teaspoon ground cinnamon**

1 **teaspoon grated lemon peel**

2 **tablespoons unsalted butter, cut into small cubes**

1 **egg beaten with 1 teaspoon water**

Coarse sugar

161

Grand Finales

Nothing impresses like an extravagant, indulgent, beautiful dessert and nothing makes it easier to create one than your KitchenAid® stand mixer. Chocolate Ravioli with White Chocolate Sauce is so delicious and so beautiful it's guaranteed to cause gasps of delight when you serve it to lucky guests. With the Ravioli Maker creating perfect little pillows is as easy as turning the handle.

Chocoholics can satisfy cravings with luscious Chocolate Cappuccino Tarts or Chocolate Hazelnut Cake. You won't have to fly to Paris or spend a fortune at the bakery to enjoy delicate French macarons, either. Chances are you'll turn out mini masterpieces on the first try with the wire whip and our tested recipes.

Get ready to establish your reputation as a dessert diva.

163

Chocolate Ravioli with White Chocolate Sauce

MAKES ABOUT 6 SERVINGS

CHOCOLATE PASTA DOUGH

- **2 cups all-purpose flour, divided**
- **¼ cup unsweetened cocoa powder**
- **¼ cup powdered sugar**
- **¼ teaspoon kosher salt**
- **3 eggs**
- **1 tablespoon vegetable oil**
- **½ teaspoon vanilla**

FILLING

- **1½ cups ricotta cheese**
- **3 tablespoons honey**
- **⅓ cup ground walnuts (optional)**

WHITE CHOCOLATE SAUCE

- **½ cup heavy whipping cream**
- **1 tablespoon unsalted butter**
- **8 ounces white chocolate, chopped**
- **1 teaspoon vanilla**
- **Fresh raspberries (optional)**

1 For pasta dough, attach flat beater to stand mixer. Place 1¾ cups flour, cocoa, powdered sugar and salt in mixer bowl; mix on low. Beat eggs, oil and vanilla in small bowl; add to mixer bowl. Mix on low until dough comes together. Replace beater with dough hook. Knead on low 5 minutes, adding remaining ¼ cup flour if needed to make smooth dough. Wrap dough in plastic wrap; let rest 20 minutes or refrigerate until ready to use.

2 For filling, combine ricotta, honey and walnuts, if desired, in medium bowl; set aside.

3 Cut dough into thirds. Flatten one piece of dough; dust with flour. Rewrap remaining dough pieces to prevent drying out. Attach Pasta Sheet Roller to mixer and set to thickness setting 1. Turn mixer to medium speed; feed dough through rollers three or more times, folding and turning each time until smooth. If dough feels sticky, dust with flour. Change to setting 2 and feed dough sheet through twice, making sure dough is as wide as rollers. Repeat at settings 3 and 4. Repeat with remaining dough. Lay finished dough sheets on lightly floured surface.

4 Replace Pasta Sheet Roller with Ravioli Maker. Fold one dough sheet in half. Fit folded end of dough between rollers and rotate handle one quarter turn just until rollers catch dough. Open loose ends of dough and drape over sides of ravioli maker.

5 Fit hopper into Ravioli Maker. Spread one spoonful of filling into hopper. Slowly turn handle, adding filling as needed. Place finished ravioli on clean cloth to dry. Repeat with remaining dough and filling. Gently separate ravioli and trim edges.

164

6 Bring large pot of water to a boil. Meanwhile, make White Chocolate Sauce. Place cream and butter in small saucepan. Heat over low heat until cream simmers. Pour over chocolate in medium bowl; stir until smooth and melted.

7 Add ravioli to boiling water; cook 3 to 4 minutes or until barely tender. Serve warm with White Chocolate Sauce. Garnish with raspberries.

French Macarons

Chocolate Macarons

1 cup powdered sugar

²/₃ cup blanched almond flour

3 tablespoons unsweetened cocoa powder

3 egg whites, at room temperature*

¹/₄ cup granulated sugar

Chocolate Ganache, Pistachio Filling (page 168), chocolate-hazelnut spread or raspberry jam

For best results, separate the eggs while cold. Leave the egg whites at room temperature for 3 or 4 hours. Reserve yolks in refrigerator for another use.

1 Place powdered sugar, almond flour and cocoa in food processor. Pulse 2 to 3 minutes or until well combined into very fine powder. Scrape bowl occasionally so ingredients do not stick in corners. Sift mixture twice. Discard any large pieces remaining in sifter.

2 Attach wire whip to stand mixer. Place egg whites in mixer bowl; whip on high until foamy. Gradually add granulated sugar, beating on high 2 to 3 minutes or until mixture forms stiff, shiny peaks, scraping bowl occasionally.

3 Add half of sifted flour mixture to egg whites. Stir with spatula to combine (about 12 strokes). Repeat with second half of flour mixture. Mix about 15 strokes more by pressing against side of bowl and scooping from bottom until batter is smooth and shiny. Check consistency by dropping spoonful of batter onto plate. It should have a peak which quickly relaxes back into batter. Do not overmix.

SHAPING AND BAKING MACARONS

4 Line two baking sheets with parchment paper. Double baking sheets by placing another sheet underneath each to protect bottom of macarons from burning. (Do NOT use insulated baking sheets.)

5 Attach ¹/₂-inch plain piping tip to pastry bag. Scoop macaron batter into bag. Pipe 1-inch circles onto prepared parchment about 2 inches apart. Rap baking sheet on flat surface to remove air bubbles and set aside. Repeat with remaining batter. Let macarons rest uncovered until tops harden slightly. This takes from 15 minutes on dry days to an hour in more humid conditions. Gently touch top of macaron to check. When batter does not stick, macarons are ready to bake.

continued on page 168

166

6 Meanwhile, position rack in center of oven; preheat oven to 375°F.* Place one sheet of macarons in oven. After 5 minutes reduce heat to 325°F. Bake 10 to 13 minutes, checking at 5-minute intervals. If macarons are browning too quickly, cover loosely with foil and reduce oven temperature slightly. Repeat with remaining baking sheet.

7 Cool macarons on pan on wire rack. If they appear to be sticking to parchment, lift parchment edges and spray pan underneath lightly with water. Steam will help release macarons.

8 Prepare desired fillings. When macarons are completely cool, match same size cookies; spread bottom macaron with filling and top with another. Macarons will keep, well wrapped and refrigerated for 4 or 5 days. Freeze for longer storage.

*Oven temperature is crucial. Use an oven thermometer, if possible.

● **MAKES 16 TO 20 MACARONS**

Chocolate Ganache: Place 4 ounces chopped semisweet or bittersweet chocolate in shallow bowl. Heat 1/2 cup heavy whipping cream in small saucepan until bubbles form around edge of pan. Pour cream over chocolate; let stand 5 minutes. Stir until smooth.

Pistachio Filling: Place 1/3 cup (1 1/2 ounces) pistachios and 1 cup powdered sugar in food processor. Process 2 to 3 minutes or until a coarse paste forms, stopping occasionally to scrape bowl. Add 6 tablespoons softened butter and 1/2 teaspoon vanilla. Pulse to combine.

Pistachio Macarons

1 Place pistachios in food processor. Pulse about 1 minute until coarsely ground. Do not overprocess or a paste will form. Add powdered sugar and almond flour to processor bowl. Pulse 2 to 3 minutes or until well combined into very fine powder. Scrape bowl occasionally so ingredients do not stick in corners. Sift mixture twice. Discard any large pieces remaining in sifter.

2 Attach wire whip to stand mixer. Place egg whites in mixer bowl; whip on high until foamy. Gradually add granulated sugar, beating on high 2 to 3 minutes or until mixture forms stiff, shiny peaks, scraping bowl occasionally.

3 Add half of sifted pistachio mixture to egg whites. Stir with spatula to combine (about 12 strokes). Repeat with second half of pistachio mixture. Mix 15 strokes more by pressing against side of bowl and scooping from bottom, until batter is smooth and shiny. Check consistency by dropping spoonful of batter onto plate. It should have a peak which quickly relaxes back into batter. Do not overmix. Follow directions for shaping, baking and filling macarons on page 166.

● **MAKES 16 TO 20 MACARONS**

¹/₃ **cup unsalted shelled pistachios**
1¹/₂ **cups powdered sugar**
²/₃ **cup blanched almond flour**
3 **egg whites, at room temperature***
¹/₄ **cup granulated sugar**
2 **or 3 drops green paste food coloring**
Chocolate Ganache or Pistachio Filling (page 168)

*For best results, separate the eggs while cold. Leave the egg whites at room temperature for 3 or 4 hours. Reserve yolks in refrigerator for another use.

169

Raspberry Macarons

1¹/₂ **cups powdered sugar**
  1 **cup blanched almond flour**
  3 **egg whites, at room temperature***
  ¹/₄ **cup granulated sugar**
  1 **tablespoon raspberry liqueur**
    Red paste food coloring
    Raspberry jam or Chocolate Ganache (page 168)

*For best results, separate the eggs while cold. Leave the egg whites at room temperature for 3 or 4 hours. Reserve yolks in refrigerator for another use.

1 Place powdered sugar and almond flour in food processor. Pulse 2 to 3 minutes or until well combined into very fine powder. Scrape bowl occasionally so ingredients do not stick in corners. Sift mixture twice. Discard any large pieces remaining in sifter.

2 Attach wire whip to stand mixer. Place egg whites in mixer bowl; whip on high until foamy. Add liqueur and food coloring. Gradually add granulated sugar, beating on high 2 to 3 minutes or until mixture forms stiff, shiny peaks, scraping bowl occasionally.

3 Add half of sifted flour mixture to egg whites. Stir with spatula to combine (about 12 strokes). Repeat with second half of flour mixture. Mix about 15 strokes more by pressing against side of bowl and scooping from bottom until batter is smooth and shiny. Check consistency by dropping spoonful of batter onto plate. It should have a peak which quickly relaxes back into batter. Do not overmix. Follow directions for shaping, baking and filling macarons on page 166.

170

Strawberry Crêpes

1 Chop half of strawberries; place in medium bowl and sprinkle with 2 tablespoons sugar. Set aside.

2 Attach wire whip to stand mixer. Place flour, eggs, milk, butter and salt in mixer bowl; whip until combined. Cover and refrigerate at least 1 hour.

3 Whisk batter until blended. Brush 7-inch skillet with oil. Heat over medium heat. Add 3 tablespoons crêpe batter, tilting skillet to cover bottom evenly.

4 Cook 1 to 2 minutes or until firm and golden. Turn; cook 1 minute or until cooked through.

5 Stack crêpes between waxed paper squares to prevent sticking together. Repeat with remaining batter, oiling skillet occasionally. Chill clean mixer bowl and wire whip.

6 Attach wire whip to mixer; beat cream on high until stiff peaks form. Stir in chopped strawberries and accumulated juice. Spoon about 2 tablespoons of mixture down center of each crêpe and roll up. Cover; refrigerate until ready to serve.

7 Process remaining strawberries and 2 tablespoons sugar in food processor until smooth. Drizzle over crêpes.

1 **quart fresh strawberries, divided**

¹/₄ cup sugar, divided

³/₄ cup all-purpose flour

3 **eggs**

1 **cup milk**

3 **tablespoons butter, melted**

¹/₂ teaspoon salt

2 **tablespoons vegetable oil**

1 **cup heavy whipping cream**

171

Butter Almond Ice Cream with Amaretto Caramel Sauce

MAKES ABOUT 1¹/₂ QUARTS

ICE CREAM

¹/₄ **cup (¹/₂ stick) butter**

1¹/₄ **cups (about 5 ounces) sliced natural almonds**

3 **cups half-and-half**

6 **egg yolks**

1 **cup sugar**

³/₄ **teaspoon almond extract**

¹/₂ **teaspoon vanilla**

SAUCE

1 **cup sugar**

¹/₄ **cup water**

1 **cup heavy cream, heated**

2 **tablespoons butter, thinly sliced**

2 **tablespoons amaretto** *or* ¹/₂ **teaspoon almond extract**

Pinch of salt

ICE CREAM

1 For ice cream, melt butter in small heavy saucepan over medium heat. Bring to a boil and cook until 3 minutes or until butter turns light brown. Pour brown butter into small bowl, leaving any burnt on specks in saucepan.

2 Preheat oven to 350°F. Spread almonds on baking sheet. Bake 10 minutes or until almonds are fragrant and lightly browned, stirring occasionally. Drizzle 2 tablespoons melted brown butter over almonds and toss to coat. Let cool.

3 Combine half-and-half and remaining brown butter in medium saucepan; heat over medium heat until bubbles begin to form around edge of pan, stirring frequently. Remove from heat. Whisk yolks and sugar in large bowl 1 minute or until pale and thickened. Gradually whisk in hot half-and-half. Pour mixture back into saucepan and cook over medium-low heat, stirring constantly with wooden spoon, until custard lightly coats spoon and instant-read thermometer reads 185°F. Strain custard though fine mesh sieve into bowl to remove lumps. Stir in almond extract and vanilla. Refrigerate at least 2 hours or until well chilled.*

4 Attach frozen Ice Cream Maker bowl and dasher to stand mixer. Turn mixer to stir; pour cold mixture into bowl with mixer running. Continue to stir 20 to 30 minutes or until consistency of soft-serve ice cream. Stir in buttered almonds.

5 Transfer ice cream to airtight container and freeze several hours.

To cool more quickly, place custard bowl in larger bowl of ice water. Let stand 1 hour or until chilled, stirring frequently.

SAUCE

6 For sauce, combine sugar and water in heavy medium saucepan. Cook over high heat, stirring until sugar dissolves. Cook without stirring 3 to 5 minutes or until caramel is copper colored and smoking, brushing down crystals that form on inside of pan with pastry brush dipped in cold water and swirling pan occasionally. Remove from heat. Gradually stir in heavy cream until smooth (sauce will boil up). Return to medium heat; stir in butter until melted. Stir in amaretto and salt. Let cool to room temperature.

7 Serve ice cream topped with sauce.

Pomegranate & Orange Sherbet

MAKES ABOUT 1¹/₂ QUARTS

²/₃ cup sugar

2 cups bottled pomegranate juice

1 cup fresh orange juice*

2 teaspoons grated orange peel

2 tablespoons grenadine liqueur (optional)

If desired, juice 3 medium oranges with Citrus Juicer attachment.

1 Bring sugar and ²/₃ cup water to a boil in small saucepan over high heat, stirring to dissolve sugar. Boil 5 minutes or until syrup is slightly thickened. Cool slightly.

2 Combine pomegranate juice, orange juice, orange peel and grenadine, if desired, in medium bowl. Stir in sugar syrup. Refrigerate 2 hours or until well chilled.

3 Attach frozen Ice Cream Maker bowl and dasher to stand mixer. Turn mixer to stir; pour cold mixture into bowl with mixer running. Continue to stir 20 to 30 minutes or until consistency of soft-serve ice cream.

4 Transfer sherbet to airtight container and freeze several hours until firm.

174

Fancy Fudge Pie

1 Preheat oven to 375°F. Combine wafer crumbs and melted butter in small bowl. Press onto bottom and up side of 9-inch pie pan. Bake 5 minutes. Cool completely on wire rack.

2 Place chocolate chips in small microwavable bowl. Microwave on HIGH 1 minute. Stir until smooth. Cool slightly.

3 Attach flat beater to stand mixer. Place brown sugar and melted butter in mixer bowl; beat on medium until light and fluffy. Add eggs, one at a time, beating well after each addition. Stir in melted chocolate, pecans, flour, vanilla and espresso powder. Pour into crust.

4 Bake 30 minutes or until set. Cool completely on wire rack. Cover and refrigerate 2 hours or until ready to serve. Garnish with whipped cream and drizzle with chocolate syrup.

1 cup chocolate wafer crumbs
1/3 cup butter, melted
1 1/3 cups (8 ounces) semisweet chocolate chips
3/4 cup packed brown sugar
1/2 cup (1 stick) butter, softened
3 eggs
1 cup chopped pecans
1/2 cup all-purpose flour
1 teaspoon vanilla
1/2 teaspoon instant espresso powder
Sweetened Whipped Cream (page 5)
Chocolate syrup (optional)

• 175

Chocolate Hazelnut Delight

CAKE

- **1 package (2¼ ounces) chopped hazelnuts**
- **2 cups cake flour**
- **½ cup unsweetened cocoa powder**
- **1½ teaspoons baking soda**
- **1 teaspoon baking powder**
- **1 teaspoon salt**
- **1 cup (2 sticks) butter, softened**
- **1 cup packed light brown sugar**
- **½ cup granulated sugar**
- **3 eggs**
- **4 squares (1 ounce each) unsweetened chocolate, melted**
- **1 teaspoon vanilla**
- **1 cup milk**
- **½ cup warm water**

FROSTING

- **1 cup (2 sticks) butter, softened**
- **4 cups powdered sugar**
- **¼ cup milk**
- **1 teaspoon vanilla**
- **1 jar (13 ounces) chocolate hazelnut spread**
- **16 whole toasted hazelnuts (optional)**

1 For cake, preheat oven to 350F. Spray three 9-inch round cake pans with nonstick cooking spray. Line bottoms with parchment paper. Spread hazelnuts on baking sheet. Bake 7 minutes or until lightly browned and fragrant. Place on clean kitchen towel; rub hazelnuts with towel to remove skins. Finely chop.

2 Whisk cake flour, cocoa, baking soda, baking powder and salt in medium bowl until well blended. Stir in hazelnuts; set aside.

3 Attach flat beater to stand mixer. Beat 1 cup butter, brown sugar and granulated sugar in mixer bowl at medium speed about 5 minutes or until light and fluffy. Add eggs, one at a time, beating well after each addition. Beat in melted chocolate and 1 teaspoon vanilla. Add flour mixture alternately with milk, beating well after each addition. Beat in warm water. Pour batter evenly into prepared pans.

4 Bake 30 minutes or until toothpick inserted into centers comes out clean. Cool in pans on wire rack 10 minutes. Remove from pans and peel off parchment. Cool completely on wire rack.

5 For frosting, beat 1 cup butter in mixer bowl until creamy. Beat in powdered sugar until light and fluffy; beat in ¼ cup milk and 1 teaspoon vanilla. Add hazelnut spread; beat until smooth.

6 Place one layer on serving plate and spread with frosting. Repeat with remaining layers. Frost top and side of cake. Pipe 16 rosettes around cake and top each with one whole hazelnut, if desired.

Pumpkin Spice Cake

**MAKES 10 SERVINGS
(ONE 2-LAYER CAKE)**

$^3/_4$ cup (1$^1/_2$ sticks) butter, softened
1$^1/_2$ cups granulated sugar
3 eggs
1$^1/_2$ cups solid-pack pumpkin
1 cup buttermilk
2$^3/_4$ cups all-purpose flour
1 tablespoon baking powder
1$^1/_2$ teaspoons baking soda
1$^1/_2$ teaspoons ground cinnamon
$^1/_2$ teaspoon salt
$^1/_4$ teaspoon ground allspice
$^1/_4$ teaspoon ground nutmeg
$^1/_8$ teaspoon ground ginger
Vanilla Maple Frosting (recipe follows)

1 Preheat oven to 350°F. Grease and flour two 9-inch round cake pans.

2 Attach flat beater to stand mixer. Place butter and granulated sugar in mixer bowl; beat on medium until light and fluffy. Add eggs, one at a time, beating well after each addition.

3 Combine pumpkin and buttermilk in medium bowl.

4 Sift together dry ingredients; add to butter mixture alternately with pumpkin mixture, beating well after each addition. Pour evenly into prepared pans.

5 Bake 40 to 45 minutes or until toothpick inserted into centers comes out clean. Cool in pans on wire racks 10 minutes. Loosen edges and remove to racks to cool completely.

6 Prepare Vanilla Maple Frosting; fill and frost cake.

Vanilla Maple Frosting

1 cup (2 sticks) butter, softened
1 teaspoon vanilla
$^1/_2$ teaspoon maple flavoring *or* 3 teaspoons pure maple syrup
4 cups powdered sugar

1 Attach flat beater to stand mixer. Place butter in mixer bowl; beat on medium until light and fluffy. Add vanilla and maple flavoring; mix until well blended.

2 Gradually add powdered sugar, beating until light and fluffy.

Chocolate Cappuccino Tarts

MAKES 4 DOZEN TARTS

Chocolate Short Dough
(recipe follows)

4 ounces cream cheese,
softened

1/2 cup sweetened condensed
milk

1 egg

1/2 teaspoon instant coffee
granules

11/2 cups cold heavy whipping
cream

1/4 cup powdered sugar

1/2 teaspoon vanilla

Ground cinnamon

Chocolate-covered coffee
beans (optional)

1 Prepare Chocolate Short Dough.

2 Remove dough from refrigerator; let stand 5 minutes. Spray 48 mini (1³/₄-inch) muffin cups with nonstick cooking spray.

3 Roll out one disk of dough ¹/₈-inch thick. Cut out circles with 2¹/₂-inch round or fluted cookie cutter. Place in muffin cups, pressing dough against bottom and sides. Press together any cracks. Repeat with remaining dough and scraps to make 48 circles. Refrigerate 30 minutes.

4 Preheat oven to 350°F. Prick holes in bottom of each tart with fork. Bake 8 minutes.

5 Attach flat beater to stand mixer. Place cream cheese and sweetened condensed milk in mixer bowl; beat until smooth. Beat in egg and coffee granules until combined. Spoon filling into tart shells. Bake 6 to 8 minutes or until filling is set. Cool on wire rack; refrigerate. Chill mixer bowl and wire whip.

6 Just before serving, attach cold wire whip to mixer. Place cream in cold mixer bowl; whip on high until soft peaks form. Add powdered sugar and vanilla; beat until stiff peaks form. Pipe 1 tablespoon whipped cream on each tart. Dust with cinnamon and garnish with coffee beans. Store covered in refrigerator.

Chocolate Short Dough

³/₄ cup (1¹/₂ sticks) butter, slightly softened

³/₄ cup sugar

3 egg yolks

1 teaspoon instant coffee granules

1 teaspoon vanilla

1¹/₂ cups all-purpose flour

¹/₄ cup unsweetened Dutch process cocoa powder*

¹/₄ teaspoon salt

Natural unsweetened cocoa powder may be substituted. Dutch process cocoa powder has a stronger flavor and will bake a darker color.

180

1 Attach flat beater to stand mixer. Place butter and sugar in mixer bowl; beat on medium 1 minute. Beat in egg yolks, coffee granules and vanilla until well blended. Scrape down bowl. Sift together flour, cocoa and salt. Add all at once; mix until just combined.

2 Shape into two disks; wrap in plastic wrap and refrigerate at least 1 hour or until firm.

Spicy Pumpkin Pie

MAKES ONE 9-INCH PIE

Pie Pastry for One-Crust
Pie (recipe follows)

1 can (15 ounces) solid-pack
pumpkin

³/₄ cup packed light brown
sugar

2 teaspoons ground
cinnamon

³/₄ teaspoon ground ginger

¹/₂ teaspoon ground nutmeg

¹/₄ teaspoon salt

¹/₈ teaspoon ground cloves

¹/₈ teaspoon ground red
pepper

4 eggs, lightly beaten

1 cup half-and-half

1 teaspoon vanilla
Sweetened Whipped Cream
(page 5)

1 Prepare pastry. Preheat oven to 400°F.

2 Attach flat beater to stand mixer. Place pumpkin and brown sugar in mixer bowl; beat on medium until blended. Stir in cinnamon, ginger, nutmeg, salt, cloves and red pepper. Add eggs; mix well. Gradually stir in cream and vanilla, mixing until combined. Pour into crust.

3 Bake 40 to 45 minutes or until knife inserted near center comes out clean. Cool on wire rack. Serve warm topped with whipped cream.

Pie Pastry

2¹/₄ cups all-purpose flour

³/₄ teaspoon salt

¹/₂ cup shortening, well chilled, cut into pieces

2 tablespoons butter, well chilled, cut into pieces

5 to 6 tablespoons cold water

1 Attach flat beater to stand mixer. Place flour and salt in mixer bowl; mix on low about 15 seconds. Cut in shortening and butter on low until mixture resembles coarse crumbs.

2 Continuing on low, add water 1 tablespoon at a time until ingredients are moistened and dough begins to hold together. Divide dough in half. Pat each half into smooth ball and flatten slightly. Wrap in plastic wrap. Chill in refrigerator 15 minutes.

For One-Crust Pie: Roll one half of dough to ¹/₈-inch thickness between sheets of waxed paper. Fold pastry into quarters. Ease into 8- or 9-inch pie plate and unfold, pressing firmly against bottom and sides. Fold edge under. Crimp as desired. Add desired pie filling. Bake as directed. Freeze remaining dough; thaw in refrigerator before using.

182

For Two-Crust Pie: Trim pastry even with edge of pie plate. Add desired pie filling. Roll out second half of dough; place on filling. Seal edge, crimp as desired and cut slits for steam to escape. Bake as directed.

For Baked Pastry Shell: Fold edge under; crimp as desired. Prick sides and bottom with fork. Bake at 450°F 8 to 10 minutes, or until lightly browned. Cool completely on wire rack and fill.

Alternate Method for Baked Pastry Shell: Fold edge under; crimp as desired. Line shell with foil and fill with pie weights or dried beans. Bake at 450°F 10 to 12 minutes or until edges are lightly browned. Remove pie weights and foil. Cool completely on wire rack and fill.

Strawberry Chocolate Roll

MAKES 8 TO 12 SERVINGS

3 eggs, separated

$1/2$ cup sugar

5 ounces semisweet chocolate, melted

$1/3$ cup water

1 teaspoon vanilla

$3/4$ cup all-purpose flour

1 teaspoon baking powder

$1/2$ teaspoon baking soda

$1/4$ teaspoon salt

Unsweetened cocoa powder

$1/2$ cup seedless strawberry jam

2 pints strawberry ice cream,* softened

For recipe, see page 144.

1 Preheat oven to 350°F. Line 15×10-inch jelly roll pan with foil, extending foil 1 inch over ends of pan. Grease and flour foil.

2 Attach flat beater to stand mixer. Place egg yolks and sugar in mixer bowl; beat on medium until light and fluffy. Beat in melted chocolate. Add water and vanilla; mix until smooth. Sift flour, baking powder, baking soda and salt into small bowl. Add to chocolate mixture; stir to combine.

3 Attach clean mixer bowl and wire whip to stand mixer. Add egg whites; beat on high until soft peaks form. Gently fold in chocolate mixture. Pour into prepared pan.

4 Bake 8 to 9 minutes or until toothpick inserted into center comes out clean. Carefully loosen sides of cake from foil. Invert cake onto towel sprinkled with cocoa. Peel off foil. Starting at short end, roll up warm cake with towel inside. Cool completely on wire rack.

5 Unroll cake and remove towel. Spread cake with jam. Spread ice cream over jam, leaving a $1/4$-inch border. Roll up cake. Wrap tightly in plastic wrap or foil. Freeze 1 hour or until ready to serve. Allow cake to stand at room temperature 10 minutes before cutting and serving.

184

Attachment Index ● THE COMPLETE KITCHENAID STAND MIXER COOKBOOK

Recipe Index ● THE COMPLETE KITCHENAID STAND MIXER COOKBOOK

Recipe Index ● THE COMPLETE KITCHENAID STAND MIXER COOKBOOK

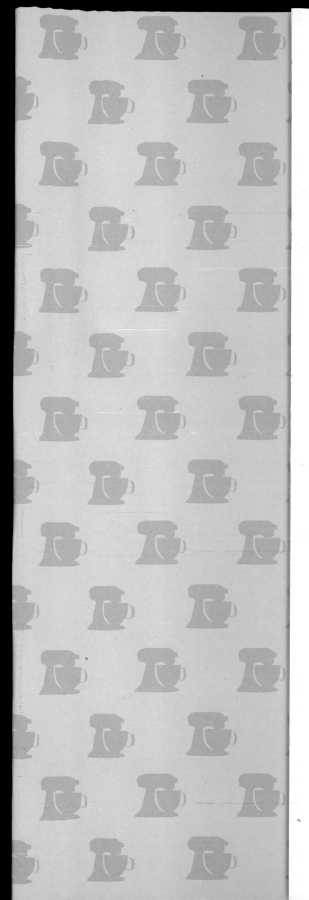

Metric Conversion Chart

VOLUME MEASUREMENTS (dry)

⅛ teaspoon = 0.5 mL
¼ teaspoon = 1 mL
½ teaspoon = 2 mL
¾ teaspoon = 4 mL
1 teaspoon = 5 mL
1 tablespoon = 15 mL
2 tablespoons = 30 mL
¼ cup = 60 mL
⅓ cup = 75 mL
½ cup = 125 mL
⅔ cup = 150 mL
¾ cup = 175 mL
1 cup = 250 mL
2 cups = 1 pint = 500 mL
3 cups = 750 mL
4 cups = 1 quart = 1 L

VOLUME MEASUREMENTS (fluid)

1 fluid ounce (2 tablespoons) = 30 mL
4 fluid ounces (½ cup) = 125 mL
8 fluid ounces (1 cup) = 250 mL
12 fluid ounces (1½ cups) = 375 mL
16 fluid ounces (2 cups) = 500 mL

WEIGHTS (mass)

½ ounce = 15 g
1 ounce = 30 g
3 ounces = 90 g
4 ounces = 120 g
8 ounces = 225 g
10 ounces = 285 g
12 ounces = 360 g
16 ounces = 1 pound = 450 g

DIMENSIONS

1/16 inch = 2 mm
⅛ inch = 3 mm
¼ inch = 6 mm
½ inch = 1.5 cm
¾ inch = 2 cm
1 inch = 2.5 cm

OVEN TEMPERATURES

250°F
275°F
300°F
325°F
350°F
375°F
400°F
425°F
450°F

BAKING PAN SIZES

Utensil	Size in Inches/Quarts	Metric Volume
Baking or Cake Pan (square or rectangular)	8×8×2	2 L
	9×9×2	2.5 L
	12×8×2	3 L
	13×9×2	3.5 L
Loaf Pan	8×4×3	1.5 L
	9×5×3	2 L
Round Layer Cake Pan	8×1½	1.2 L
	9×1½	1.5 L
Pie Plate	8×1¼	750 mL
	9×1¼	1 L
Baking Dish or Casserole	1 quart	1 L
	1½ quarts	1.5 L
	2 quarts	2 L

192

191

Metric Conversion Chart

VOLUME MEASUREMENTS (dry)

⅛ teaspoon = 0.5 mL
¼ teaspoon = 1 mL
½ teaspoon = 2 mL
¾ teaspoon = 4 mL
1 teaspoon = 5 mL
1 tablespoon = 15 mL
2 tablespoons = 30 mL
¼ cup = 60 mL
⅓ cup = 75 mL
½ cup = 125 mL
⅔ cup = 150 mL
¾ cup = 175 mL
1 cup = 250 mL
2 cups = 1 pint = 500 mL
3 cups = 750 mL
4 cups = 1 quart = 1 L

VOLUME MEASUREMENTS (fluid)

1 fluid ounce (2 tablespoons) = 30 mL
4 fluid ounces (½ cup) = 125 mL
8 fluid ounces (1 cup) = 250 mL
12 fluid ounces (1½ cups) = 375 mL
16 fluid ounces (2 cups) = 500 mL

WEIGHTS (mass)

½ ounce = 15 g
1 ounce = 30 g
3 ounces = 90 g
4 ounces = 120 g
8 ounces = 225 g
10 ounces = 285 g
12 ounces = 360 g
16 ounces = 1 pound = 450 g

DIMENSIONS

1/16 inch = 2 mm
⅛ inch = 3 mm
¼ inch = 6 mm
½ inch = 1.5 cm
¾ inch = 2 cm
1 inch = 2.5 cm

OVEN TEMPERATURES

250°F = 120°C
275°F = 140°C
300°F = 150°C
325°F = 160°C
350°F = 180°C
375°F = 190°C
400°F = 200°C
425°F = 220°C
450°F = 230°C

BAKING PAN SIZES

Utensil	Size in Inches/Quarts	Metric Volume	Size in Centimeters
Baking or Cake Pan (square or rectangular)	8×8×2	2 L	20×20×5
	9×9×2	2.5 L	23×23×5
	12×8×2	3 L	30×20×5
	13×9×2	3.5 L	33×23×5
Loaf Pan	8×4×3	1.5 L	20×10×7
	9×5×3	2 L	23×13×7
Round Layer Cake Pan	8×1½	1.2 L	20×4
	9×1½	1.5 L	23×4
Pie Plate	8×1¼	750 mL	20×3
	9×1¼	1 L	23×3
Baking Dish or Casserole	1 quart	1 L	—
	1½ quarts	1.5 L	—
	2 quarts	2 L	—